Learn What Y[...] [...]g to Tell You- [...]'t!

You think *you* have problems? Try being three. You have a million questions, yet grown-ups get tired of answering them; you're constantly made to try new foods when your favorites are just fine; and nearly every time you attempt to do something for yourself, like get dressed or pour a glass of water, someone tries to help you. To make matters worse, whether you're happy, sad, tired, or angry, you have difficulty expressing in words how you're feeling.

In this revolutionary approach to understanding a three-year-old, child development specialist Dr. Jerri Wolfe allows you to see life through your child's eyes. Each entertaining and enlightening entry identifies a common behavioral problem, presents your child's perspective of it, and then offers a variety of sensible solutions—allowing you and your child to form a bond of communication and friendship that could last a lifetime.

I'm Three Years Old!

I'm Three Years Old!

by ME

Everything Your Three-Year-Old Wants You to Know About Parenting

As Told to Jerri Wolfe

becker & mayer!
BOOKS

POCKET BOOKS

New York   London   Toronto   Sydney   Tokyo   Singapore

This book is a work of fiction. Names, characters, places and incidents are products of the author's imagination or are used fictitiously. Any resemblance to actual events or locales or persons living or dead is entirely coincidental.

An *Original* Publication of POCKET BOOKS

POCKET BOOKS, a division of Simon & Schuster Inc.
1230 Avenue of the Americas, New York, NY 10020

Copyright © 1998 by Jerri Wolfe

A becker & mayer! book, Kirkland, Washington
www.beckermayer.com

All rights reserved, including the right to reproduce this book or portions thereof in any form whatsoever. For information address Pocket Books, 1230 Avenue of the Americas, New York, NY 10020

ISBN: 0-671-00337-2

First Pocket Books trade paperback printing October 1998

10 9 8 7 6 5 4 3 2 1

POCKET and colophon are registered trademarks of Simon & Schuster Inc.

Cover design by Patrice Kaplan
Cover photo by Bob Thomas/Tony Stone Images
Interior illustrations by Ty Pollard
Text design by Stanley S. Drate/Folio Graphics Co. Inc.

Printed in the U.S.A.

TO

my mother, Edie Mulkey

Acknowledgments

My heartfelt thanks to:

Karen Joslin, who thought of me when this project was first being developed.

Andy Mayer and Jim Becker, who recognized the importance of understanding the child's perspective.

My husband, Mike Johnson, for creative thinking and late-night proofreading.

Jennifer Johnson, my daughter, and her friends Nathan, Hillary, Kevin, Taylor, Mikela, Hayden, Andrea, and Micah. While sharing your third year of life I became wiser.

Ingela Hense, Linda Heard, Matt King, Debbie Patashnik, Julie Smith, and Alissa Seidlitz, my cohorts in parenting, for walks, talks, flowers, and many hours of child care.

The dedicated parents who have attended my classes at Northwest Hospital and Overlake Hospital and whom I have worked with in the Parent Education Program at Bellevue Community College. Your experiences and questions have given to me a greater understanding of young children.

Contents

Introduction

As a parent I see my daughter and the world through a parent's eyes. That's only natural. Shortly after Jennifer's third birthday, I was embarrassed by her pronouncement that the lady in front of us in line was fat. I felt frustrated and exhausted when she forgot to use the bathroom. Later, after reading two stories and saying good night to every stuffed animal known to man, I got angry when she refused to go to sleep because of the monsters.

What should I do? That's a question I get asked over and over again while teaching parenting classes. How can I get my child to behave? How can I get him to be "good"? Frustrated, embarrassed, angry, and exhausted parents come to my parenting classes hoping for a miracle cure to an ageless malady. But before we can hope for a cure we must examine the source of children's behavior. Why do so many three-year-olds have what seem to be unreasonable fears? Why are they sometimes so incredibly stubborn? And why is it so tough to get them to stop what they're doing and come to the dinner table?

Children do not cause us problems just to make us crazy. They behave like children because they *are* children. They don't think the way we do, they

1

have less experience in the world, and they have fewer skills. When a three-year-old says, "That lady is really fat," she is not meaning to be rude, only verbalizing an observation. When my daughter refuses to go to sleep because of the monsters, it's because they are real to her, or at least she thinks they might be. Hadn't I been the one who read her those stories about princesses, giants, and monsters? And though I have years of experience using the toilet, my three-year-old is still learning to use the potty.

It is not easy moving from an adult perspective into the mind and heart of a child. It may be impossible to be a three-year-old and appreciate the parent's perspective. We can make the switch, they can't. The results can be very powerful. Instead of seeing a child choosing to make your life difficult, you will see a child who is struggling to learn about her world and attempting to develop the skills of being a big kid.

Most of us don't remember how we felt and behaved at age three. The children in *I'm Three Years Old!* will remind us what we have forgotten and help us understand. This book is organized into seventy-three short stories addressing specific issues. The children will tell you in words we can understand why they behave the way they do, how they are feeling, and what they need from us as parents. They will tell you that being three is different from being two, that they are big kids now. While the book is written in a child's voice, it certainly goes beyond the words and thought processes of the three-year-old. It is their hope and mine that this information will help you move beyond the frustration, anger, and desire to punish that we as parents often feel. Instead you will ask yourself, What do I need to teach my child so that he can be more successful? Understanding the child's perspective helps us to work with our children rather than to force our will upon them. The first part of the miracle cure is understanding children; the second is acting on that knowledge. Good luck.

ACTIVITY LEVEL

I am not good at watching. I need to move,
but lots of time when I do I get in trouble.

No, not Ashley's swimming lesson again. I don't want to go to Ashley's swimming lesson. You won't let me do anything but sit. I would like to play in the water puddles in the locker room, push the button on the hair dryers, and climb on the bleachers. But you say "No," "Be good," "Stay right here and don't touch anything," and "Sit still." I can't just do nothing! My body just has to move. I need to touch things, to climb, and to run. How can you just sit there and watch?

I AM A DOER NOT A WATCHER. WHAT I NEED YOU TO DO IS:

Don't fight my activity, plan for it.

Please don't ask me to do something I can't do. Please bring something for me to do. When we go out to eat you always bring some crayons and windup animals. I love it when you wind up the yellow bunny and we watch it flip over. Maybe I could pack some windup animals or my trucks in my

5

backpack and take them to the swimming pool. Do you think I could drive my trucks on the bottom bleacher? Ashley's swimming lessons are long. I might not be able to play alone with my trucks that long. Would you play with me? It's more fun and the time goes by more quickly. When we go into the locker room it would help if you told me two things I could do. I wish I was taking swimming lessons. Do you think there is a class for me at the same time as Ashley's?

Plan for breaks for yourself.

I have a lot of energy and I require a lot of your energy. For me to be successful I need you to think ahead, keep a close eye on me, and play with me and give me lots of hugs. Whew, that's a bunch of things. Some days you say I have worn you out. I'm sorry. Just think when I'm a little older I can use my energy to swim on a team or play soccer. But for now I think you need a little time-out. Maybe Jessica from next door could come over and play with me while you take a rest.

Aggression

*I wanted that shovel, but when I reached
for it Erin made a face at me and took
it. She made me so angry I poured
sand on her head!*

I am a doer, I love to run, climb, swing—to use my whole body. When I need a ball, a truck, or some more Play-Doh I use my body then, too. You say "No hitting or no grabbing, use your words." You tell me I am a bad boy, that if I keep behaving this way no one will want to play with me. But the words don't come first, the action does. Yelling at me, putting me in time-out, and spanking me lets me know how angry you are, but it doesn't help me learn to stop the bad actions. Please help me learn, I do want to have friends.

Focus on amends, not punishment.

I think Erin was crying after I poured sand on her, but I'm not sure because you took me away and started yelling. If you want me to understand why pouring sand is bad you need to let me see Erin crying. I need to see the sand in her eyes and in her hair. It would even help if Erin told me "Don't do that it hurts." Tell me that I hurt Erin and that I will need to do something to make her feel better. Please don't yell. If you use your calm voice it will be easier for me to listen. Maybe I could get a towel for her or say I was sorry.

Keep your eye on me.

I don't have good self-control yet, so I need you to help me stay in control. Sometimes all I have to do is look at you and you tell me with your face that I need to stop. It seems I have the most problems when no grown-ups are around to help or when grown-ups are busy talking to each other. When you see me start to grab for the trike Zack is on, don't just say "stop," ask me what will happen if I push Zack off the trike. I need lots of practice thinking about my actions. Help me see that I have choices. I could push Zack and take the trike, I could look for another trike or toy to play with, I could ask Zack if I could have a turn, or I could ask Zack if I could push him on the trike.

Please hug me, don't hit me.

I learn more from your actions than your words, I'm an action kind of kid. You tell me no hitting, no grabbing, and then you hit and grab me. You say use your words but lots of times when I do you don't listen. Please listen, and help me learn about feelings. Tell me when you are angry and show me how to take deep breaths to get rid of the yucky angry feelings inside. Hug me and let me know that you love me even when I'm feeling angry. It is hard to learn self-control, if you work with me instead of against me it will be a lot easier.

Anger (CHILD'S)

I hate Peter, he has my balloon and he won't give it to me. I hate him!

Stop that! You do not hate your brother. You know you love him. A balloon is not worth all this fussing. Go in your room until you can come out with a better attitude." Why am I getting in trouble? Peter took my balloon! When I was two I would have kicked him and grabbed for my balloon, but you always say use your words. I am using my words! Why won't you listen to me? Why won't you help me? Do you think that being sent to my room will make me feel better? It won't.

PLEASE DON'T PUNISH ME FOR BEING UPSET. WHAT I REALLY NEED IS FOR YOU TO:

Let me be angry.

Why do you get so upset when I get angry? I can tell you like me much better when I am happy. I don't try to get angry, it's just that there are so many things that aren't the way I want them. Does that ever happen to you? I need to hear that everyone gets angry sometimes. Tell me about how you got angry when the paperboy threw the newspaper on the roof.

Help me express my anger in okay ways.

I want to make the bad feelings go away. If I hit Peter and got back my balloon that would make me feel better. But you say the rule is no hitting. I am trying to follow the rule. What should I do? I said I hated Peter because I hate the way I feel inside when he won't give me my balloon. I'm not sure exactly what *hate* means but I know it's a strong word. I need to know that what I am feeling is frustration and anger at Peter for not giving me my balloon. It would be better if I said "Peter, you make me so angry!" Words can help the angry feelings go away.

Let me know that sometimes it takes more than words to get rid of the angry feelings. Help me learn to get calm inside. Maybe we could cuddle and read a book, go for a walk, or blow some bubbles. Thanks for helping me, I couldn't learn this by myself.

ANGER (PARENTS')

Stop this instant! No hitting! How many times have I told you not to hit your brother? What am I going to do with you? When are you going to start listening to me? You are impossible!

I was playing with the animals and then Michael came over and took the fence I was using. I yelled, "Give that back," and then I hit him. That's what you do when you get angry, you yell and then you hit. Michael makes me so angry sometimes. You say "No hitting" and then you hit me. I'm confused.

IT WOULD HELP IF YOU WOULD:

Show me how to be in control
of my anger.

You say the rule is no hitting, then what am I supposed to do? You say use your words, but the words you use hurt. It would be easier for me to hear your anger if you kept it simple. You could say "It makes me angry when I see you hitting your little brother." Tell me that you are taking ten deep breaths to help you get calm inside. Then we will talk about my problem with Michael.

Tell me you love me.

I make you angry a lot. It must be because I am impossible, whatever that is. I think it has something to do with being three. I'm sorry. I get so scared when you get angry. Do you still love me? Help me learn that people can be angry at each other but still love each other. Could you just hold me, please?

Take care of yourself.

Are you feeling sick? When I'm sick I get real grumpy, and you are pretty grumpy. Maybe you need to lie down and take a nap. Or you could get a baby-sitter and go visit with your friends. You always seem happier after you've gotten to play with your friends.

Baby-Sitters

No, please don't leave me. I want to go, too!

Why won't you take me? I want to go where you go. Why do I have to stay home? I don't like it when I'm not with one of you, you are my parents. I need you! When are you coming back? Please don't tell me that I'm acting like a baby. I am not a baby, I'm a sad three-year-old.

I DON'T LIKE BEING LEFT. SOME WAYS YOU CAN HELP ME WITH THIS INCLUDE:

Get me a really good baby-sitter.

Erika plays dolls with me, she lets me paint, and one time we had a tea party. When I am sad she asks me if I want to sit and read for a while or if I want to do something silly. She smiles and laughs a lot and tells me funny stories. That other baby-sitter, the one with the long hair, she doesn't know how to play. She just says "What video do you want to watch?" She doesn't talk to me, she just sits and watches TV. I don't think she likes me. I don't think she likes being a baby-sitter. If I have to have a baby-sitter, please get Erika.

14

Share my sadness with me.

You want me to be happy that Erika is coming to baby-sit me. I like Erika, it's just that I like my parents the best of all. I don't know why you can't be with me all the time. I make a fuss because I want you to know how I feel. When you say "Stop that fussing" I cry even louder. You are not listening. What would help is if you would sit with me and tell me you know how hard it is for me to be left. Having you close and knowing that you understand helps me to feel better.

Be sure and say good-bye.

You think that maybe it would be better if you just snuck out while Erika and I are in my room. It wouldn't. That would be really scary. I need to say good-bye. Our special family good-bye helps me to feel loved. So please don't forget our group hug and kiss. Then Erika and I will stand at the door and watch you honk the horn and flash the lights. Good-bye! I'll miss you.

BAD HABITS

Michelle! How many times do I have to tell you to quit picking at your lips!

I'm sorry, Mommy. I didn't know I was doing it. Please don't yell, it makes me all upset inside. Being three and a half is hard. You used to do everything for me, but now I have to put my pajamas on and pick up my toys. And there are lots of rules for me to remember. Don't pick up the dog. No standing or jumping on the sofa. Always hold hands in parking lots. There are so many things, I just don't know if I can do it all!

When I was a baby I used my pacifier to help me feel better. Now when I feel upset I pick at my lips, chew on my hair, or chew on my blanket. These things help me feel better . . . until you start to yell. Why can't you just leave me alone? Can't you see I'm having a hard time already?

SOME WAYS YOU CAN WORK WITH ME ON THIS INCLUDE:

Gently help me break my habit.

Don't pick at your lips!" "Quit doing that!" Why do you get so upset when I pick at my lips? I don't understand. I need you to show me that my lips get ouchies on them when I pick at them. I'll try not to pick, Mommy, but most of the time I do it without thinking. Tell me that you will help me quit by reminding me when you see me doing it. But please don't yell. Instead just say "lips" in your quiet voice.

Cuddle more, yell less.

Don't just tell me what not to do, tell me what I *can* do! I feel yucky a lot, and I need a way to help me feel better. What do you do when your insides are all upset? Show me how you take really deep, slow breaths. At preschool I feel better after I play with Play-Doh or bubbles, maybe I could do that at home, too. And I always feel better after we have cuddled, but we don't cuddle much anymore. I'd like it if instead of yelling at me you would say "It looks like you're having a hard time, would you like to cuddle?"

Bathroom Language

Stop it! You poo-poo head!

When I was two you said, "No biting, use your words." Now I am using my words. I am learning that words can be powerful. Tara stopped squirting me with water when I called her a poo-poo head. Why did you tell me to stop talking that way? I am not hitting, biting, kicking, or grabbing, I am using my words.

Words can be fun, too. Sometimes when my friend Sam and I are riding in the car I say poo-poo head and he says doo-doo face, then we laugh and laugh. You tell us to stop, but we don't stop, we like being silly, and when you're driving you can't do anything to make us stop. *Poo-poo head* is my favorite word. I can use it when I want to be silly and when I want to feel powerful. When I say poo-poo head I get a lot of attention.

YOU DON'T LIKE POO-POO HEAD, I DO. HERE'S HOW TO WORK WITH ME ON THIS:

Ignore it.

The more attention I get for using poo-poo head the more I use it. It makes me feel in control. If I don't get attention when I use it, I guess I will find another word to get your attention.

Teach me acceptable strong words.

A three-year-old can use words instead of their body to express how they feel. I call you a poo-poo head when you won't give me a cookie or when you turn off the TV before my show is over. Sometimes you make me so angry. You put me in time-out and say we don't use bad words. If I can't say poo-poo head when I am angry at you, what can I say? Can I say butt head? That's what Tommy's big brother says when he gets angry. Can I say godammit? That's what you said when the dog chewed on the rug. Tell me that we all need strong words sometimes, to say how we feel. Words like *poo-poo head* and *butt head* aren't okay to use because they hurt people's feelings. When I need a strong word I can try these: "Darn it!" "Don't do that!" "Stop it!" "You make me so mad!"

Help me have fun with words.

I say words because I like to hear the way they sound. I like long words like *stegosaurus* and *tyrannosaurus rex* and I like it when you read books with rhyming words. Sam and I like to be silly with words. We use bathroom words because we are both learning to use the potty but we can be silly with other words, too. You could suggest we think of silly food words, like *mashed potatoes, spaghetti,* or *zucchini.* If you don't like hearing bathroom words maybe Sam and I could go into the bathroom and say them, that's what our teacher tells us to do when we have the bathroom-word sillies at preschool.

Bedtime Battles

Mom, I need another sip of water. I need to go to the bathroom. Dad, I forgot to give you a hug.

Going to sleep was easy when I was in my crib. I would cuddle with my blanket, snuggled against the side of the crib. My crib was special, it felt so safe. But I am a big kid now with a big-kid bed. Bedtime starts out good, you help me with the big three—teeth brushing, hair brushing, and going potty. Then it's off to my room for night clothes and two stories. I used to beg for more stories but you said no, the rule was two stories. Pleading for more stories didn't get me more stories so after several attempts I quit trying, I get two stories. I like having a routine for getting ready for bed, that way I know exactly what is going to happen next. I know that I get three kisses, because I am three, and then you say good night and leave the room. That's when the trouble begins. You want me to stay in bed and go to sleep. It's not that easy. Part of me wants to go to sleep but the other part wants to be with you. What are you doing? I'd like you to be with me. Could you get me a drink of water? I need my stuffed bear. Will you help me find it? I hear a noise outside my window, I'm scared. When I was in my crib I didn't have the choice to leave my room, now I do.

I AM HAVING TROUBLE STAYING IN BED. WAYS YOU CAN HELP ME INCLUDE:

Help me get prepared to stay in bed.

You can't make me go to sleep but you can help me stay in bed. I am learning how to get to sleep in this big bed, it's just not the same as my crib. It is hard to go to sleep when I'm not in bed. Before I get in bed for stories, ask me to find the animal I am going to sleep with, get a cup of water for my nightstand, and check for any bad guys under the bed and in the closet. Be patient while I get my space in order, but be aware that in an attempt to keep you longer I will ask for things I don't really need. What I really want is you. You can put an end to my stalling by asking me what is the one last thing I need to do before stories.

Tell me that I am to stay in my bed after you leave and that you will come and check on me in five minutes. I will relax, knowing you will be back soon. If I am still awake in five minutes, come in and give me a kiss and then ask me if I want you to come again in five or ten minutes. I feel secure knowing you are near.

Don't yell, it wakes me up.

I know you want me to stay in bed, but I just couldn't control the urge to find out what you are watching on TV. I'm sorry, please don't yell. When you yell, it scares me, and I get even more awake. Then it is really hard to get to sleep. In your calm voice remind me that I am to stay in bed, take my hand, and walk me to my room. Tuck me in and say "I'll check on you in five minutes, I promise."

BIRTHDAY PARTIES

Scott invited me to his birthday party.
He and I are friends.

I have been to Scott's house before but never with so many other kids. I wanted to play with trucks. Scott and I always play with trucks together, but Scott won't play with me. He was talking to a kid I didn't know. When we sat at the table for cake I wanted to sit next to Scott, but those chairs were already taken. Then we sang "Happy Birthday to You" and Scott blew out the candles. Scott got mad because one of the other kids blew a candle out, so his mother lit them again. This time Scott blew them out all by himself. The cake was chocolate with white frosting and purple and green trucks on it. It was really good. Then Scott started opening his presents. I like the bulldozer that I got for Scott. I wish I had one. I am not sure I can give this to Scott. Do you think Scott will let me play with it? It's hard giving presents.

I AM JUST LEARNING ABOUT BIRTHDAY PARTIES.
IT WOULD HELP IF YOU WOULD:

Tell me what to expect.

Before I go to the party please tell me that at a birthday party there are lots of exciting things like decorations, cake, candles, singing, and presents. Because the birthday person has invited several friends he won't be able to play with me like when I come to play. Let me know that you know how hard it is for me to give presents that I really like. Remind me that when it is my birthday people will give me presents. I want a bulldozer just like the one I gave Scott.

Teach me some birthday manners.

At Scott's birthday party kids were jumping on the sofa, running and screaming through the house. Scott's mom didn't seem very happy. I need to hear that sometimes kids get excited at birthday parties and forget the rules. Ask me what the rules are when we are inside the house. If I say them to you I am more likely to remember them at the party. Okay, the rules are, no running in the house, chairs are for sitting not standing, and use my inside voice when I'm in the house. When it's time to leave remind me to say thank you to the birthday person and to his parents. If I am a good guest maybe they will invite me over again soon.

Let me help plan my own party.

I want a cake just like Scott's with trucks all over it and I want truck cups and plates. Please take the presents from kids as they come and put them in a high place. At Scott's party some of the kids opened the presents that they brought and started playing with them. It would be good if my party wasn't too long, just a little time to play, then cake and presents. After I open my presents put them back into a high place, I don't want anyone playing with them. Since they are new they are special and I want to have some time with them by myself. Help me say good-bye and thank you for coming when my friends leave. I will likely be busy and won't think of it on my own.

Biting

You say "Use your words." I did use my words! No one would listen.

I said "Stop that" and "Quit pushing me," but the kids keep pushing. I felt trapped. I don't like being all crowded in with other kids. I wanted out, but we were supposed to wait for the teacher to tell us it was okay to go outside. I just couldn't take it. I didn't plan to bite Riley, he just kept pushing me. Now everyone is mad at me. I'm sorry, Mommy, I didn't mean to bite. I must be bad. Biting is bad and sometimes I bite.

I WANT TO BE GOOD. IT WOULD HELP
IF YOU WOULD:

Stop yelling. It doesn't help.

Please stop yelling. I know biting makes you angry, but yelling only makes me more upset. Yelling doesn't help me understand what happened or teach me other ways to handle my frustration. If you need to be sure I know the rule, ask me, "What is the rule about biting?" and "Why do we have this rule?"

Don't ask why. Ask what happened.

Don't ask me why I bit him, I'm not sure myself, it just happened. You could help me understand why by helping me think about what was happening just before I bit him. First help me calm down, I can't think when I'm upset. Please use your calm voice, when you are calm it's easier for me to get calm. Now ask me what I was doing before I bit Riley. What was Riley doing? Tell me that you are glad to hear that I tried to solve the problem by telling Riley to stop. Let me know you understand how frustrated I must have been when I kept getting pushed. Let me know that you don't like being all crammed in with other people either. Knowing that you understand and share my problem makes me feel better and want to hear more. When you get all crowded in what do you do? You don't bite, do you? Explain that first you say "Please don't push," but if the pushing continues you get out of line. I could get out of line. I could move to the back of the line. And if the teacher asks what I'm doing I can tell her that I was being pushed so I am moving to the back, away from the pushing.

Bossiness

I have lots of ideas about playing princess and now I have the words to tell Hillary exactly how I want it to be. I expect that she will do everything the way I want it.

Put the teacups here, and the plates go right there. No! Don't put the spoon there, it goes here. You can wear the green dress, I'll wear the gold one. Hillary, stop doing that! I'm supposed to wear the pink crown, you can have the flower one. I get so frustrated when Hillary won't play princess right.

Why do you think I'm bossy? I am telling Hillary what to do and how to do it just like you tell me. You say "It is time to get your clothes on" and "First, put your arms in and then head. Next put your pants on." Isn't that how relationships work?

I'M JUST LEARNING HOW TO PLAY WITH OTHER CHILDREN. IT WOULD HELP IF YOU WOULD:

Practice the art of compromise with me.

I am just starting to understand that other people have ideas, too. When I was two, I only knew what I wanted. When you told me it was time to come in the house for dinner, I said no. Now when you say it's time to come in the house I say "Please let me drive my car around the yard one more time!" How about a little compromise? It would make both our dinners better if you would.

Prepare me for a little give-and-take.

I get so excited when I know that Hillary is coming over. I have so many ideas about what I want to play. I'm so busy thinking about my ideas that I forget that Hillary might have ideas, too. Suggest after Hillary gets her coat off that I ask her what she would like to do.

Don't interfere if we are using our words.

Hillary wants to wear the pink crown. She says that she won't play princess if I won't let her wear the pink crown. I yell, "No, it's mine!" Now I have to decide what to do. If you step in and solve the problem, Hillary and I will learn that you have all the answers. Then we will come to you when we have problems. If you leave us alone I will have to decide which I want more—to play princess or to wear the pink crown. Learning to compromise is hard but I won't learn if I never have the opportunity. Don't be too far away when you hear yelling, though. If I get too frustrated I might start hitting and I will need your help to get back in control.

After Hillary leaves be sure to tell me what a nice job I did of sharing my toys. Remind me that when I share and let Hillary decide what we're going to play, she has a good time and will want to come back.

Chores

Look at me, I'm washing the car! Can a baby do this? I can. It makes me feel good to be doing grown-up things.

I've seen you clean the mirrors before, but until now I wasn't very interested. Now I would like to understand what you are doing and I would like to try it. Teach me how to spray the cleaner on the mirror and give me my own paper towel to wipe it up. Can I do it again? This is fun. What else can I help you with? Can I stir the toilet cleaner with the brush? Put the soap in the washer? Water the flowers?

Why do you get so grumpy when you are cleaning? You seem to be in such a hurry. Why don't you want my help? I'd like to help you dust. I will do the best job a three-year-old with limited experience dusting can do. You say "Go look at a book" or "If you want to help go clean up the toys in your bedroom." You don't get it, I want to be with you. I need you to show me how to care for our things. I can't go clean up my room. There are so many toys I won't know where to begin.

I WANT TO HELP YOU. HERE IS WHAT I WOULD LIKE YOU TO DO:

Let me be your assistant.

Don't miss the opportunity to include me in the cleanup duties. I am volunteering now. If you dampen my helping spirits I might not be so eager to help when I'm older. So please let me be your assistant. Let me feed the dog, put the mail in the mail box, and sort the socks. We can make chores fun. I'll race you to the mailbox. After we're done working I love to hear "Monica, the mirror looks beautiful" and "Thank you for helping me with the laundry." Being a part of the family and making you happy feels good.

Be my assistant.

I have a hard time completing a task by myself. I need an assistant who will help me to get organized and to stay focused on the task. Sometimes my room really does need to get cleaned up, not too often though, I like my toys where I can reach them. When that time comes start by asking me if I want to pick up the animals or the books. Let's see who can get theirs put away first. Show me how to take the bedding off my bed, and you and I can put it in the wash. Once my room is clean let's stand back and tell each other "Good job." Thanks, it's great to have an assistant like you. When the two of us work together the cleaning sure goes fast.

Cleaning Up Toys

I've spent all day playing in my fort and now you want me to take it down!

My favorite thing to do right now is build a fort. The best forts are made with chairs, blankets, end tables, and sofa cushions. Once I get my fort just right I arrange all my stuffed animals inside. My fort is such a magic place I never want it to go away. You would like to sit down on the sofa. But I don't want my fort disturbed!

I THINK WE CAN WORK THIS OUT. HERE'S HOW:

Give me some warning before it's time to clean up. And make it fun!

When you say "Clean up your toys" I just keep on playing. I am busy and need a warning before I

35

can even consider cleaning up. If you want me to clean up a big project like a fort or block castle I need a warning in the morning: "Tonight before dinner we are taking down the fort so I can vacuum." When it's time to clean up, it's much more fun if we make it a game. The funniest way to get the things picked up is when you put away the trucks and I put away the cars, and the fastest one wins.

Help me build my fort where it won't have to be cleaned up right away.

I love making forts with the sofa cushions, but I might be talked into a new design using the dining room table or a card table and blankets. Then you could sit on the sofa and I could still have my fort! Let's place the fort in a place that isn't in your way but is still close to the family room. I don't want to be too far away from the rest of the family. And please let me keep my fort up until I've moved on to another activity like building a great block castle.

Another way you can make cleanup easier for me is to give me boxes or trays for different types of toys, like a yellow box for small animals and a red box for plastic food.

Whatever you do, don't tell me to clean up at bedtime. I'm just too tired!

CLOTHING CHOICES

*I love my yellow pj's. You want me to wear
the red ones but I won't wear them! I like
the yellow ones best.*

Each night when I go to sleep I lie on my side with
my blankie crunched just right and my dog Fluffy
under my arm and I feel so snug. When I wear my
red pj's it just doesn't feel right. Something about
the cloth makes my skin tickle and the legs creep
up and feel wrong. I always, always want to wear
my yellow pj's.

When I was a baby you did a great job of caring
for me and dressing me. Now I'm a big kid and
clothing is part of my expression of my individual-
ity. I'm three years old and I can be pretty head-
strong at times, especially about my clothes.

HERE'S HOW TO WORK WITH ME ON THIS:

I don't care what my clothes look like.
It's how they feel.

I know you feel those red pj's should be worn, they
are the right size and you paid good money for

them. Have you ever bought clothing for yourself and then found out it wasn't all that comfortable? I bet you have jeans in your closet you don't ever wear! If I really can't wear the same pj's every night, why not buy me another pair exactly like the yellow ones? Before I wear them they'll have to be washed a few times to get them to feel just right.

It would also help if you could give me some words to describe the funny way clothes feel. That way I will be able to tell you with my words when something feels bad, rather than taking them off soon when you're not looking.

Let me decide what to wear.

I know you have specific ideas about how I should dress during the day and night, but so do I. Pretending is a big part of being three. When I look different, I'm different.

Let's not fight constantly over clothes. I don't have time for this. I want to go out and play. Why don't you just give me some simple choices? How about you select three outfits and I'll choose one?

And don't give me a hard time if I want to wear my green vest over my orange shirt. I'm experimenting with bright colors right now and those two are really bright. I'm wearing them, not you!

Here's another tip: during the winter, you could put away all of my summer clothes. That way I won't choose a short-sleeve shirt to wear when it's snowing outside. (If you don't tell me that I have summer clothes I probably won't remember.)

CRIES EASILY

Waaaaaaaaaaaaaaaaaaaaaaaaaaa!

My cry is my signal that I am having trouble. This time Renee took the red paint! Hearing my cry, you come running, pick me up, tell me I'm okay, and then find something else for me to do. I like the way you come and save me when bad things happen. All I have to do is cry.

When I was a baby, crying was one of my only ways to get your attention. Now that I'm three I use words most of the time. I still cry, though, when I get in tough situations, like when someone pushes me on the way up the slide, or grabs my toy. I haven't learned any other ways to cope.

*I NEED TO LEARN NEW WAYS TO DEAL WITH LIFE'S
FRUSTRATIONS. YOU COULD HELP BY:*

Quit rescuing me.

You always help me to calm down at least for the moment. But each time you rescue me I feel helpless and more sure that I need you to save me from the bad kids and the bumps and bruises in the world. You don't like my cries and focus on trying to get me to stop. That's not what I really need. What I need is some encouragement that I can handle bad things.

Teach me to be assertive.

I think Renee has learned that if she wants my toy she can just take it because I will cry, and you will take me somewhere else. I am getting a lot of attention by being a victim, and Renee gets what she wants. I need to learn to tell Renee no, but I'm scared, so I cry. I might feel a little braver if you would stand by me. I could cry, you would come, then ask me if I want to tell Renee the rule about taking toys or if I want you to tell her. Then tell me to tell her what I want her to do. "Give it back!" That felt better. Maybe if I said no more to Renee she wouldn't take my toys.

Don't call me a crybaby!

You are not very nice to me when I get an ouchie. You say "Quit being a crybaby! You're okay." I'm not okay, it hurts. You wonder why Michelle doesn't cry when she gets a bump. I don't know, doesn't she feel the pain? You can help me get in control by asking me to show you where I got hurt. Sometimes it's not the ouch that is causing me to cry. I don't know why I'm just all upset inside. Hearing "I bet you felt scared when you got pushed" helps me to understand what I am feeling. That's it, I was scared, now I can start to feel better. Could you please give my knee a mommy kiss? Can I go back and play now?

DEATH

What is dead? When will Fluffy wake up?
I want to play with her.

Fluffy and I are friends. She likes her ball, and when I pet her nicely she purrs. But she's not purring now. What's wrong with Fluffy? Why are you crying, Mommy? Did something bad happen? Did I do something bad?

PLEASE, I NEED TO KNOW WHAT HAPPENED.
I NEED YOU TO:

Explain what *dead* means.

You told me that Fluffy died, but I don't know what that means. I need you to tell me that when an animal dies its body stops working and stops moving. Fluffy doesn't need to eat, sleep, or breathe because she isn't alive anymore. Tell me that everything that lives—like plants, animals, and people—dies. Some things live for a very short time like some bugs, and others like people live for a very long time.

I am pretending my stuffed animals are dead and then alive and then dead again. My play is where I work on hard things like *dead*. I can tell dead is important, but I don't really understand it. When I watch cartoons people get squished and then they pop back up. When will Fluffy just stand up and be alive again? Why does she have to be dead? Is this bug dead? When will Mariah's cat die? For a while I will be asking a lot of questions about death. I may ask the same question over and over again. Please be patient, I am just trying to understand. Let's go to the library and see if there are any stories about a cat dying. That would help.

Help me say good-bye to Fluffy.

Fluffy and I liked to do lots of things together. I miss Fluffy. Do you miss Fluffy, too? Tell me that when someone we love dies we feel sad. That one way to feel better is to say good-bye and to remember the good times you had together. Help me make a good-bye card. We could put a picture of Fluffy on it and we could write the things she liked to do on it. Then we can write good-bye. Good-bye is hard.

DEFIANT

No! I don't want to! You stupid-head!

No, no, no! You think I'm saying this just to make you angry. You're wrong. I have a certain way I like things and when things aren't that way it feels bad. It's like when socks don't fit just right my whole body goes crazy. And I feel that way when things change quickly or there are too many new things. I say no because I'm overwhelmed and I am trying to protect myself from the bad feelings.

IT WOULD HELP IF YOU WOULD:

Help me even when I call you stupid-head.

Getting angry and yelling "Don't talk to me that way" doesn't help, it hurts. I may be saying "No! You stupid-head" but what I really need is your help. I can't wear this sock this way, don't try to force it on me. I will fight you. What I need to hear is "Something about this sock is causing you problems, can you show me what it is?" Help me learn the words to describe the problem, then next time I can say "Stop, the seam is not right."

Help me anticipate change.

I have a lot of trouble leaving places, like the park or my friend Peter's house. Maybe before we go, say "Last time we were at the park you made quite a fuss when it was time to leave. Let's think of a better way to leave this time." I think it would be better if you came over to me and told me we were leaving in five minutes. Then you could ask me what one thing I would like to do that would help me get ready for leaving. Lastly I would like it if you would give me a piggyback ride to the car. Yeah, I think it will work, let's try it.

Early Riser

When I wake up early I get to watch all my favorite TV programs. Mooom, I'm awake!

I am awake and I want you to get up. You make a funny noise and say "Go back to sleep it's too early to be awake." I can't, I am awake and I'm hungry, too. Why are you so grumpy when you wake up?

YOU SEEM TO NEED MORE SLEEP THAN I DO. I MIGHT SLEEP LONGER IF YOU WOULD:

Give me a nighttime snack.

It's a long time between dinner and morning. I wake up hungry. I might sleep longer if I had a snack before I went to bed. A glass of milk and a banana sound good. What do you think?

Teach me the good morning rule.

You want me to sleep longer. Why should I? Look what I get when I wake up early—TV, breakfast, and sometimes I get to snuggle with you in your bed. My body wakes up when it is done sleeping. If you don't want me to wake you up, what can I do?

Maybe I could play with toys in my room. You could help me choose some books and toys to put by my bed. In the morning they would be right there for me. Tell me that now that I am three I can have my own clock in my room. This is a very special clock, it knows just the right time for getting up and will let me know by playing music. So when I hear the music I will know that it is time for everyone to wake up and I can come and say good morning to you. Could I get in and snuggle now?

Another tip: I hear you talking and watching TV after I've gone to bed. If you really need a lot of sleep, go to bed earlier.

Eating

Look, Dad, Grandma didn't eat all of her vegetables. Tell her she can't have any dessert until she eats all of her broccoli!

I don't like dinnertime. I can't just eat, you watch every bite I take. If I'm really enjoying my potatoes you interrupt with "Now it's time to eat some of your carrots." Then you say "No dessert unless you eat your meat." The meat must be bad if you have to give me something in order to eat it. Finally, you force me to take three more drinks of milk, even though I am already full. Why can't you just let me decide what I'm going to eat and how much?

LET'S MAKE DINNERTIME BETTER. IT WOULD HELP IF YOU WOULD:

> Put healthy food on the table and then leave me alone.

Some days I am not very hungry, I just don't feel like eating. Please don't force me to eat. I am listening to my body, it says no. When I was learning to use the potty you told me to listen to my body

49

for the signs that I need to go. Why can't I listen to what my body tells me about food? Yesterday carrots tasted good, today they don't, I don't know why but the rice tastes good today. If you're worried that I'll choose to fill up on junk foods, then don't make them available. My body also tells me when it's time to stop eating. Don't make me eat more than my body needs! It feels yucky to be too full. It can't be good for me to eat too much.

Don't call me picky.

Grown-ups eat a lot of yucky foods. I don't like foods mixed together or covered with sauce and I don't like things that smell or look different. You say "Quit being so picky, it all gets mixed together in your stomach" or "Just try one bite." No, you might be able to make me put it in my mouth, but I won't swallow it. I am not picky, I'm just not ready to try those foods. Maybe after I see these foods several times and watch you eat them, I'll get the courage to try them. But if you call me picky, and tell Grandma I don't like things, like green beans, then I will become picky and decide that I must really not like them. Being picky sure gets me a lot of attention.

I use the word *yuck* a lot when it's mealtime. It says just what I feel. Why do grown-ups get so upset when they hear "yuck"? Is there a better way to talk about food? Explain to me that there are words that I can use that sound better than *yuck*. Tell me that if I am offered a food that I don't like I can say "No thank you, I don't want any."

Plan regular meal and snack times.

You get angry when I ask for a snack right after dinner. You say "If you had eaten dinner you wouldn't be hungry" and then you give me some cheese and apple. Why should I eat dinner if I can get good food after I leave the table? I might eat a better dinner if I knew I couldn't get food soon after. Why not give me cheese and apple with dinner, it's much better than that yucky mixed-up food you serve some days. Even when I eat a good dinner I get a little hungry before I go to bed. It would be good if I could count on having a snack after bath.

Let me help.

I am learning about eating and food. I like to cook. When you made banana bread I gently cracked the egg, held the cup while you filled it with flour and sugar, and stirred all the things together. Cooking food makes me feel grown-up. I liked it that you told me I could be an official taster just like Dad. It is the job of the official taster to tell you just how good the things are that we have made. I like to make muffins, bread, and especially cookies. I can also wash vegetables, tear lettuce, and butter bread.

EATING OUT

*At home I come to the table when the
food is ready, I eat, and then I get down
to play. When we eat out, I have to sit for
a long time until the food comes, and
then after I eat I have to sit some more.*

How can you sit and just talk? Doesn't your body
need to move? Don't you see the ice cubes floating
in your water and want to catch one with your
spoon? Don't you see those little containers on the
table and wonder what is in them? You glare at me
when I slide down in my seat and tell me to sit
up. How am I supposed to sit up? These seats are
slippery and don't fit my body. Why do we have to
eat out? It's no fun.

IF WE HAVE TO EAT OUT IT WOULD HELP IF YOU
WOULD:

Pick a restaurant that knows kids, not just grown-ups.

The perfect restaurant for me would let you sit down right away, no waiting. I prefer booths, and booths by windows are really good. As soon as I sit down the worker would bring me some food. The food would be good, things I've had before. I don't like trying new things in strange places. This restaurant would have all its lights on and I would be allowed to talk in my regular voice, not my quiet voice. When I finish eating, the worker would give us our bill so we could leave. Or better yet they would have a play area where I could go while you talk. On the way out I would get to pick what color of balloon I wanted to have. Now that would be a good place!

Plan activities for waiting times.

You tell me what not to do. "Don't blow into your straw." "Don't play with the ice cubes." "Stop making that noise with your fork." The only do's you have are "Sit up in your chair" and "Use your quiet voice." I just can't sit and wait. I need to do something. I could color if the restaurant has some crayons. What I would really like is if you would color with me. Talk to me about the pictures and the colors. I will tell you what things I want you to color. Not all restaurants have crayons so we should bring our own. Other things that we could do while we wait are read a book and play with a small windup toy. I'm not good at waiting on my own, I really do need your help.

EMBARRASSING QUESTIONS AND REMARKS

That man has no hair. What happened to his hair? I don't like it, it looks ugly.

I see a lot of things around me. (After all, I'm only three!) Many things I know, but some things I've never seen before. When I see different or strange things I ask about them. Most of the time you smile and give me an explanation. Just yesterday you explained why some people wear glasses, why Grandma's chocolate chip cookies taste different from the ones we make, and why some men have hair on their face. Sometimes when I ask questions or say something your face gets all funny-looking and you say "Shhh! We're not to talk about it!" Or you say that I'm not nice. I don't get it. I'm not a bad girl, I'm just trying to understand.

HERE IS WHAT I THINK WE SHOULD DO:

I'll whisper my questions in your ear.

Since I don't know which questions are going to hurt other people's feelings maybe I could whisper my questions in your ear. I think whispering is

56

really fun. If I have a comment about another person I could whisper that to you.

I need answers to my questions.

I'm really trying to make sense of the things around me. When you don't answer my questions I get all mixed up. If you can't answer my question right now, tell me that you will explain it to me later.

EMPATHY

Go away! We don't want to play with you.

Becky and I are playing. We are both horses and we like to run through the wading pool and splash water. Mom, Luke is standing too close to the pool. Make him go away. You say "Be nice to Luke." But Mom, he is in our way.

YOU TELL ME TO BE NICE A LOT. I'M NOT SURE HOW TO DO THAT. I NEED YOU TO:

Help me think about other
people's feelings.

Telling me to be nice is not enough, I need you to help me be nice. Tell me that it looks like Luke wants to play. Toddlers think big girls are really neat and it would make him very happy if I let him play for a while. Suggest that I include Luke by asking him if he wants to be a horse, too. Then remind me how good it feels when Hillary lets me play with her and her friends.

Be respectful of my feelings.

It's hard having a little brother. He's always in the way. You want me to be nice and to think about his feelings, but what about my feelings? When I got angry because Luke knocked over my fort you said "Stop that" and sent me to my room. And when Luke got paint on my picture you told me to calm down, "it was no big deal." I need you to listen and think about my feelings. Instead of telling me to be nice I need to hear "It's hard to have a little brother some days." Tell me that you know how angry I get sometimes. Knowing that you really understand how I feel helps me. Now I feel good enough to let Luke play with us.

Involve me in caring for others.

When we took cookies over to Dan's house he got a big smile on his face and said I was his special friend. I like Dan, and I like it when we do things for other people. I am learning that thinking about other people is a good thing. Look, Mom, a pinecone, I am going to save this for Luke. He really likes cones.

Fearless

I am curious, I like to try new things and I need to move.

Why did I climb to the top of the playhouse? I needed to see what was up there. Why did I ride my tricycle down the big hill? I wanted to see if I could do it. Why did I let go of the swing? I wanted to see what would happen. My body feels best when it is working hard to try something new. Sometimes, though, I get hurt when I play. Why did that have to happen? Please, make my arm stop hurting.

You tell me I need to settle down, that I won't get hurt if I would think before I do things. Think about what? That's why I did it, it seemed like a good idea. I wanted to slide upside down and backward. Don't you? Most of the time I don't get hurt, only sometimes. I can't settle down, that would be like not doing anything. How will I know which things I do are dangerous and which are not?

I NEED YOU TO HELP ME TO BE SAFE. HERE ARE SOME THINGS YOU CAN DO:

Provide safe but challenging activities.

Some days I hear "no" all day. No climbing, no running, no jumping. I need some yeses. Take me to a place where it is okay to climb. Sign me up for a gymnastic or swimming class where I can try all kinds of new things. The teachers will help me learn to follow directions. I need excitement every day. If we have to stay home, build me an obstacle course, bring my slide in the house, or show me what happens when you mix vinegar and baking soda. Teach me how to climb well, how to be good at it and how to be safe.

Teach me to think ahead.

Mostly I live in the moment, I get an idea, and then I try it out. You can help me learn to be safe by teaching me some simple safety rules, like climbing only when a grown-up is there to help or always wearing a helmet when riding a tricycle. Help me remember the rule by asking "What is our rule about climbing?" Sometimes I will need help remembering.

Help me think ahead but still enjoy what I'm doing. Stay by where I am, that way you can help me make good decisions. Then if I look like I'm thinking about going down the hill on my tricycle you can ask me "Do you think riding down the hill with your feet off the pedals is a good idea? What might happen if you do that? What can you do instead so that won't happen?" It is hard for me to think of these things on my own, but with your help and lots of practice I can learn. Pushing myself feels good. I just can't stop from trying things but I can learn to be safe.

Fears (NIGHTTIME)

It's in there. It wants to grab me!

I can't sleep in my bed, there are monsters in my room. They make scary noises and like to eat little kids. Don't tell me there is nothing to be afraid of, I saw one. You would be afraid if you saw it, too. It was big, with a big head and big hands, and they reached out to get me. You can't see it because it's hiding. It's in there, I know it!

THE MONSTERS ARE REAL TO ME. I NEED YOU TO:

Reassure me.

I am too little to fight off the monsters, I need you to protect me. I need you to tell me "Daddy is here, it's okay, you're safe." Please hold me, I feel safe in your arms.

Help me find ways to get rid of the monsters.

Help me think about these monsters. Why have they chosen my room? How do I know when they are there? What makes them scary? I could even draw a picture of the monsters, just so you would know what one looks like. Then we could think about what might scare those monsters away. Maybe they are afraid of wolves. I could put my wolf stuffed animal next to me in bed, that might keep them away. Wolfy is very brave. Maybe we could make a magical spray that would keep the monsters away or we could tie some bells on a stick and shake it at them if they get near. Let's talk to the librarian about monsters. She might know of some good books about how other children got rid of monsters.

Help me feel safe in my room.

The monsters are in my room only when it's dark. I don't like the dark. I see and hear things I don't understand. If you sit with me in the dark I can show them to you. It would be fun if we used a flashlight to make shadows on the ceiling with our hands. We could use the flashlight to explore the scary shadows in my room. Once I see where the shadow comes from I won't be afraid anymore. Can I sleep with this flashlight next to me? I don't think monsters like the light.

FEARS (OF REAL THINGS)

**No! I don't want to go outside,
there are bugs outside.**

I have seen them, bugs on my slide, bugs on the sidewalk, and bugs in the sandbox. Bugs scare me, I won't go where there are bugs. Don't tell me that I'm being silly, that bugs can't hurt me. Bugs can hurt, I know. When we went camping I got bit by a mosquito. My arm got red and it really itched. You don't like bugs, you squish them.

I am not just afraid of bugs, a lot of other things scare me, too. When I was two I didn't know that bugs bite, or that alligators can eat people. Can alligators climb out of the toilet? You look and make sure it's not there. What if I fall into water, how will I breathe? What will I do if a big dog jumps on me and bites me?

PLEASE HELP ME! I'M LITTLE, AND I'M SCARED.
I NEED YOU TO:

Respect my fear.

I am afraid. Isn't it okay to be afraid? When you call me silly or a scaredy-cat I get even more afraid. I'm too little to protect myself from all the bad things, I count on you to protect me. If you're not going to help me, who will?

Sometimes I get stuck on the things that frighten me. I need you to help me move on. It feels better when you say "Sean, I can see that you are afraid of getting your head under the water." Show me that you are not afraid of going underwater, and tell me about how you learned to swim. Tell me so that I can learn to swim, too.

Help me understand my fear.

Bugs are bad, they bite. Why did that mosquito bite me? Help me understand. I just know a little about bugs. What I know scares me. I would like it if we went to the library and got some books on bugs. Once I know more about them I might be less afraid. I need to know that there are many different kinds of bugs, that they help us and that most don't bite. It might even help if I could look at a bug in a jar with a lid. That way the bug couldn't hurt me.

Set a good example.

Whenever you see a dog, you grab me or squeeze my hand. I am learning from you that dogs are something to be afraid of. You tell me to never go near a dog. Are all dogs bad? My friend Sean has a dog that he plays ball with. I might like to play ball, too. I need to learn some safety rules about dogs, like always ask the owner if you can pet their dog before trying to touch it. Read books to me about dogs and let me watch Sean play with his dog. Then when I'm ready let me try to pet his dog. I think I can get over being afraid of dogs, but I need your help.

FRIENDS

Who am I going to play with today?

You used to be my preferred playmate, you let me decide what to play, you never took my toys, and you always let me go first. That was when I was two. Now I want, no I need, to be around other kids. I really like to play with Meagan at day care, she and I like to dress up and pretend to be princesses. Meagan and I both like the gold crown the best. I wanted to wear it today and I said "No me," but then Meagan said "Can I please wear it." It made me feel good that she said "please" so I let her wear it. Now that I am three I can consider someone else's feelings.

I AM READY AND EAGER TO MAKE FRIENDS.
YOU CAN HELP BY:

Arranging play dates for me.

Mommy, this is Meagan, she is my friend. Can Meagan come to my house? I want to show her my kitty, and my trike, and my room. I have a lot of playing energy. You think that being at day care should be enough for Meagan and me. But playing at home is different and special. Please ask Meagan's mommy if she can come over. Having a best friend is fun and makes me happy.

Being patient during the rough times.

$\mathbf{S}$top it, Meagan." "Mommy, Meagan is putting the jewels in the doctor bag, I want them in the purse." "I want Meagan to go home!" Please don't be too far away, Meagan and I need you, sometimes we have different ideas and we don't know what to do. We need you to ask each of us what we want to do with the jewels and then ask if we can think of an idea that we both like. I know having a friend over can be a lot of work for you. We interrupt a lot and you can't get your things done. But this is important. You are helping us learn how to solve problems. With a little more practice we might not need your help at all.

"We are not playing with the blocks." "No! I don't want you to touch my doll." Some days I start playing nicely, but then I start to have trouble. It takes a lot of energy to share. Maybe after a snack and a story I will feel better. Please don't make the play dates too long. I want to be good but at times I just get too tired. And don't invite more than one of my friends over at once. I just can't pay attention to that many kids.

FRUSTRATION

How would you feel if you had no choice about what you wore or how you spent your day?

I have a lot of ideas about what I like and what I want to do. So when I want to wear my red dress, have pancakes for breakfast, and go to the park and you say no, I get really frustrated. I feel frustrated a lot. It happens when I am trying to put on my shirt and I get stuck and can't get out and when I try to pour the juice and it spills. Sometimes I get so frustrated when the puzzle piece won't fit that I throw the pieces all over the floor. I wish that things would be easier and the way I want them.

BEING THREE CAN BE VERY FRUSTRATING. IT WOULD HELP IF YOU WOULD:

Give me some control.

Please let me have some choices. Instead of saying "It's time to get out of the bath" say "You can get out of the bath now or in five minutes." That way I can think about if I am ready to get out or if

I need a few more minutes. I think I'm done, I am ready to get out now.

Help me do things myself.

I am not a baby anymore, I am three, and I need to be able to do some things myself. Will you show me how to put my shirt on so my head goes into the right place? Could you put less juice in the pitcher or buy a smaller one like we have at day care so it is easier to pour? I'd be able to get my own coat and shoes if you put them where I could reach them. I need to do these things so I can become competent, independent, and responsible. So stop doing things for me that I can do for myself. And be patient, I am learning, and learning takes time. Hey look at me, I buckled my shoe.

Talk to me about frustration.

Every time I try to do the animal puzzle I get frustrated. Maybe it is just too hard for me right now. Putting it away might be a good idea. I know you like it better when I am happy. But don't protect me from all frustration. If I don't experience some frustration how will I learn new things? It was hard, really hard, to buckle my shoe, I had to try again and again. I started to get frustrated, and then I remembered how you couldn't get the lid off the pickle jar. You told me it was on tight and that you were frustrated that it didn't come off when you twisted it. You said that feeling frustrated can make you want to just quit, but that instead you take two deep breaths and then try it again. If that doesn't work you think about other ways to try. Sticking to it is good, you said. So when I got frustrated I took two breaths just like you, and it helped.

GIMMES

Mommy, can I have some animal stickers,
can I, can I, please!

I am a child who loves elephants, and whenever I see something with an elephant on it I want it. I have an elephant T-shirt, a soft stuffed elephant, little plastic elephants, but no elephant stickers. Please, Mom, can we buy them? You know how much I like elephants. It would really make me happy if you bought them for me. Please! Sometimes you buy me things and other times you say no. I have learned that no doesn't always mean you won't buy it. Asking two, three, or even four times can change a no into a yes. Why can't I have everything I want? I like new things, don't you?

I DON'T REALLY UNDERSTAND ABOUT MONEY.
IT WOULD HELP IF YOU WOULD:

Teach me about exchange.

I'm not sure what *buy* means. Sometimes you give the worker a little card, or you write on a piece of paper or you give money. If you gave me a little card I could buy my own toys. That would be good.

73

I could get whatever I want. I need to hear that when the grown-ups in our family go to work they get paid money and then we use that money to buy the things that we need. Let's set up a store, we can use some of my toys. On some toys put one sticker to show that toys in our pretend store cost one dollar. Other toys will have two stickers on them. Now give me some paper money and let's go shopping. I think I want this elephant and this dog, each has two stickers, so I need to pay you four of my dollars. Oh, oh, I only have three dollars, I will have to decide which I want more, the elephant or the dog.

Let me handle the money.

Give me a pile of coins and let me separate them into piles. Teach me the names of each: penny, nickel, dime, and quarter. When we go to the store tell me how much things cost. This pepper is one quarter, this loaf of bread is one dollar. One dollar is more than one quarter, so which costs more, the pepper or the bread? After the worker has put our groceries in the sack let me pay the money. This time she gave me some money back. Why?

Listen to my wants.

When I asked for the stickers you said in an angry voice "Why won't you ever be satisfied with what you have?" What does that mean? When I see neat things I want them. How will I know what I can have and what I can't if I don't ask? Sometimes you buy me things and other times you don't. If I ask for something and you say no, it would be much easier on me if you really meant no. Now I never know if I make a fuss if you will change your mind. Maybe you could say "No, and no matter how many times you ask the answer will still be no." I get sad when I see something I want and I can't have it. I would like it if you would ask me what I like about it. Or say "I know how much you like elephants, and these stickers have lots of elephants on them. Let's make a wish list for the things you see you wish you could have. These stickers could be the first thing on the list."

Holidays

Would you tell me again who this present is for? What about this one? And this one? How many more days until we get to open the presents?

I like presents and cookies with frosting and candy and candles and lights and decorations. I love the bells on the tree, each one makes a different ring. I put my special little mouse decoration, the bells, and the pretty clothespins dolls all in this spot on the tree, they are my favorites. I want them all together where I can look at them. Please tell me again about how you made the star when you were little and how it is always the last decoration on the tree. This is so exciting. Can I help put some more things on the tree?

I AM BEGINNING TO UNDERSTAND ABOUT HOLIDAYS. IT WOULD HELP IF YOU WOULD:

Not plan too many holiday activities.

Why do we have to get up? I don't want to go to a parade. After spending all day at Grandma's house yesterday, I just want to stay home. I want to turn on the holiday music and play with my decorations. No! You are not listening. I don't want to go. You say "Stop it, we need to get in the car." I am over-whelmed, tired, and frustrated. There is only so much holiday excitement I can handle. You wish I would quit screaming and crying. I can't. Please let's stay home.

Tell me what to expect.

You say every year our family and friends go to Aunt Christine's house for dinner, singing, and opening presents. This is my fourth year, but I don't remember going when I was a baby. You say it is important that I be a good girl while I'm there. I want to be a good girl, can you help me be a good girl? I need you to tell me when I will get to open my presents. And how instead of opening all our presents at once we take turns. After I open a present I am to look at the person who gave it to me and say thank you. That will make them feel good. Can I eat whatever I want from the pretty little bowls? Oh look, Aunt Christine has bells on her tree, can I touch them? When do we get to sing?

Prevent problems.

Matthew and I are playing chase. He is hiding from me and I am chasing after him. I hear your voice, I think you said stop running. I see you, Matthew, you can't hide from me. I think I hear your voice again, but there's a lot of noise in the room. Now I am running all over, bumping into people. I am out of control. We have been here a long time, I have eaten mostly chips, and I didn't get a nap. You are angry and say that I am not behaving. I started out okay, but it's hard to behave when I am tired. Please don't yell. Instead I need to hear "I know we have been here a long time and you are tired." If it's not time to go yet, take me to a quiet place and hold me. After I've had a little quiet time and something good to eat I might be able to join the group for singing. Next time please don't wait until I get out of control to help me. Make sure I am well rested, eat foods that will make me feel good, and give me some attention and quiet time during the day.

IMAGINARY FRIENDS

Taylor took the cushions off the sofa. I told her no, but she didn't listen to me. I am a good girl, Taylor is the bad girl.

Who is Taylor? you ask. She is my friend. You don't see Taylor, she is only in my mind. Only I can see her, and she talks only to me. She likes to go on car rides so I let her come with me, and we play together whenever I feel like pretending to be animals, we both like that. She never visits when I have other friends over, she waits until they have gone. Taylor is a great friend because she can always come and play. Don't worry, nothing is wrong with me. I am just having fun. Maybe if you knew more about Taylor you wouldn't be so concerned.

SOME IMPORTANT THINGS TO KNOW ABOUT
TAYLOR AND ME ARE:

Taylor is special to me.

You don't like Taylor. You say she is not real. That's not very nice. What is real anyway and why does it matter? You read me stories about animals that talk and wear clothes, and I watch TV shows where people fly, fight pirates, and live inside a whale. Does that stuff really happen? I don't care, it is fun to hear, to watch, and it is fun to play make-believe. I know Taylor is not like my other friends, but you can still be polite, she is my guest. When Taylor is visiting I would like it if you would say hello and let her sit at the table at lunchtime. Let me decide what is best for Taylor. She is my special friend.

Taylor helps me work on new skills.

Taylor is only two and I am teaching her about rules. I tell her that we have rules in this house, she will have to follow them when she comes to play. I told her that she can't play with the dog's toys, that we get cookies only at lunchtime, and that we have to be sitting at the table when we're eating. The problem is that she doesn't like rules. She says that rules get in the way of having fun. I had to put her in time-out when she threw a block. I told her in a strong voice "We don't throw blocks in our house." I know the rules, I am three, it's harder for two-year-olds to remember, they're still learning.

I'm sorry Taylor took the cushions off the sofa. She wanted to make a fort for the dolls. What are you going to do? You can't remind her about the rule and have her clean it up, she only hears me. I know, you can say "Tell Taylor that the rule is the cushions stay on the sofa, it will have to be cleaned up and you will do it for her." I think that will work and I will tell her that if she takes the cushions off again she won't be able to play in the living room for the rest of the day.

INDEPENDENCE

"I did it!"

Look, look at me, I've climbed all the way up to the top of the big slide. Get ready to catch me. Here I go. Wow! That was fun, I want to do it again and again. Look at that girl, she is little, she can't go on the big slide. I am a big girl and there are lots of things that I can do myself. I'm really good at taking off my clothes at bedtime and putting on my pajamas. And I can put my own toothpaste on the toothbrush. At breakfast time I like peanut butter toast. I put the toast in and push the button, and I use my special knife to spread the peanut butter. It feels so good to do it myself. Knowing that I can do big-kid stuff helps when it comes time to do really hard things like starting preschool or going to the doctor.

I AM LEARNING TO BE INDEPENDENT, BUT I NEED YOUR HELP. IT WOULD BE GOOD IF YOU WOULD:

Be patient, I'm just a beginner!

I was trying to put on my sock, stop don't do it for me. It must be hard for you to watch me do things.

It does take me a long time, and I don't always get it right. I know you can do it faster, but how will I learn if you won't let me do it? Maybe I'll learn that I shouldn't try, that I'm not big enough, that you should do everything for me. Is that what you want? If you want me to be able to do things for myself then you will have to sit with me as I struggle to learn.

Teach me how.

Shoes are very confusing. Sometimes they feel good. Sometimes they don't, and then you say I have them on the wrong feet. Could you show me a way I can remember which shoe goes on which foot? And how can you tell which is the front and the back of my panties? I need to know that. I like getting myself dressed. I wish all my dresses had big buttons in front like this one.

Let me help you.

Look, Dad, I set the table. A baby couldn't do this. I can! And I can help make the salad, put the dressing on the table, and clear my plate when I'm done. It sure is good to be three, I can do so many things.

But please don't force me to be independent. I'm still learning. Some days I just don't have the energy to be grown-up.

LISTENING

*"Sammy, it's time to come upstairs
for teeth brushing. Sammy, it's
teeth-brushing time. Sammy, get up
here this instant!"*

You think that I am choosing not to listen to you.
I'm not. I'm busy playing with my schoolhouse, and
all my attention is focused on listening to the bell
ring. When you think I'm not listening you get
angry and yell. I don't like that. Just because you
say something doesn't mean I heard it.

*IF YOU NEED ME TO LISTEN IT WOULD HELP IF
YOU WOULD:*

Make sure you have my attention.

I hear lots of things. The television, Mom talking
on the phone, and Vern next door barking. But
sometimes when I'm playing I don't hear any
sounds. If you say "Sammy, it's teeth-brushing
time" from way across the room I might not hear
you. You can make sure I hear you by getting close
to me. I would like it if you sat down by me and
listened to the bell, too. Then touch my arm gently,

and once I'm looking at you tell me it's teeth-brushing time. Can I have a piggyback ride upstairs? Here we go.

Help me remember.

Sammy, why did I send you up to your room?" I don't remember, Dad. Once I got in here I saw my sticker book and I decided to put some stickers in it. Sometimes after I have heard you, I forget what you said. It would help if you said "Sammy, go get your coat and your hat." Don't use too many words, that confuses me. Then ask me "What two things are you getting?" I remember—my coat and my hat. I'll try.

Say nice things.

You yell a lot. "Get your coat now!" "Stop making that noise!" "Sammy, I'm talking to you!" "I told you to put your toys away!" I don't like that voice, so I try not to look at you, that way I can't hear you. It's much better when you say "It's time to go, I'll go with you to get your coat" or "That noise is hurting my ears, I need you to stop." But I like it best when you say "Sammy, you are so special to me" and then give me a big hug.

Lying

"Jaykob, did you color with felt pens on your pants?" No, I did not do it!

I can tell by the sound of your voice that you are not happy. Felt pens on pants must be a bad thing. I am a good boy, a good boy only does good things, so I must not have done it. Even when you tell me you know I did it because I have felt pen on my hands, I will insist I didn't. I am just beginning to learn about right and wrong, good and bad. People who do bad things, like the bad guys on TV, are bad. I am not like the bad guys, people don't like bad guys. If I am bad you won't like me.

Please don't call me a liar. I don't know what a liar is but I can tell that it is really bad. It's just that sometimes bad things happen. I don't always know how they happen. I believe in magic and wishes, and if you wish bad things to go away they do.

I AM NOT A BAD BOY. HERE'S HOW TO WORK WITH ME ON THIS:

Focus on solutions, not blame.

When you found juice on the floor you asked "Did you do this?" I did not want to make you angry so

I must not have. The monster from my closet did it, *he* does bad things. I need you to say "Jaykob, when juice gets on the floor, the floor gets sticky, that's why we have a rule that we don't leave the table with a cup of juice. Here, let me show you what we have to do to clean it up."

Tell me mistakes happen.

I make mistakes sometimes. Mistakes make you angry. Will you still love me if I make a mistake? If I get in trouble every time I tell you about a mistake, I will learn it's not good to tell the truth. I am only three, I can't be perfect. Are grown-ups perfect? Have you ever spilled your juice? It will feel safer to tell the truth if you say "We all make mistakes sometimes. When you think that there is a problem I would appreciate it if you tell me, I will not yell at you. Next time you spill your juice, tell me, I will help you clean it up."

Reduce the temptations.

Even though I know the rule is I am not to touch the books on the table in the living room, I sometimes touch them. It's just that they are right where I can see them and they have lots of pictures in them. My desire to look is so much greater than my self-control. If you really don't want me to look at those books, put them where I can't see them so easily. I have the same problem with the cookie jar on the table. I like cookies so much that I can't seem to control the urge to take one when you are not looking, even though I know that we don't get cookies until after lunch.

It's a tall tale, not a lie!

My friend Mike and I saw a ghost in the living room. It was hiding behind the sofa. We were really quiet and we surprised it and then we put it in this bag. Then we took the bag outside and let it go. It won't come back to our house. Mike and I are very brave. You say we didn't really see a ghost, that my story is a lie. But we did see it. My imagination is so strong that the pictures I create in my mind become real to me. Lies are bad things and my stories aren't bad, they are my way of sorting out the things around me. Instead of calling it a lie call it a make-believe story, that will help me separate fantasy from reality.

MANNERS

No! I don't like peanut butter cookies;
they're yucky. Give me something else!

I don't think Sam's mother likes me. She doesn't smile at me when I come over to play. I wish she would have given us chocolate chip cookies today, I know where they keep them so I opened the cupboard and took the bag out. Sam's mother said "No, we are not having chocolate chip cookies right now. It is not polite to help yourself to food when you are visiting." She was angry. What is "polite"?

I WANT PEOPLE TO LIKE ME. I NEED YOU TO:

Please teach me what polite is.

I have learned that some words like *poo-poo head* hurt people's feelings. Now I am ready to learn the words that make other people feel good. Tell me that everyone likes to be asked for things nicely. If I want you to get me some orange juice I can say, "Mommy, orange juice, please." After I get my orange juice the polite thing to say is thank you. We can practice. You can ask me to pour you some milk, please, and then you can say thank you to me.

Teach me visiting manners.

When I'm at home and I'm hungry I just open the refrigerator and get out some carrots. Why can't I do that at Sam's house? I need you to tell me that I am a guest when I'm at Sam's house and that if I need something I need to ask a grown-up politely. If I am offered food I don't like, I should say "no thank you" rather than "yuck." When it is time for me to leave, I should say "thank you for having me" to the grown-ups and to my friend.

If Sam comes to my house then I am the host. A host can make his guest feel good by going to the door and saying "Hi! I'm glad you are here."

When Sam leaves I should go to the door and say "thank you for coming over." Wow! That's a lot to remember. Could you come to the door with me? We could say hello and good-bye together.

Do the right thing yourself.

I don't just learn words from you, I learn how to use them. When you smile and say thank you to the dry cleaner, to the grocery clerk, and to the mail carrier I see them smile back. Being polite can be very powerful. I know I like it when you are polite to me.

Masturbation

*Stop doing that! It's not a nice
thing to do.*

Stop doing what? I am just watching TV. Oh, you want me to stop rubbing my doll between my legs. Why? When I rub just right it feels good. Now that I wear big girl pants it's easy to get that good feeling. I like to do that when I watch TV, and sometimes I do it when I'm lying in bed, it helps me fall asleep.

HERE'S HOW TO WORK WITH ME ON THIS:

Teach me about private parts
and privacy.

What is the bump that I have between my legs? It tickles when I touch it. Do boys have a bump like this? I like learning about my body and how it works. I have learned about my muscles, my heart, and now I am interested in this bump. I need you to tell me that the name for that is clitoris. Tell me that boys and girls have most of the same body parts but that a few are different. Boys have a penis and girls have a clitoris and a vagina. These body parts along with the others that are covered by a swimming suit are called our private parts. They are special and are only for us to touch. Touching our private parts does feel good and is something that people do in private, with no one else around. When I want to touch my private parts I should go into my room where I can be by myself.

Morning hassles

Some mornings you wake me up by saying "Good morning, good morning, good morning" and then we cuddle. But most mornings you just say "It's time to get up" and then you pull the covers off. Brrr!

Why do we have to rush around? I like quiet cuddly mornings where I have lots of time to get dressed, brush my teeth, and play with my toys. You tell me to hurry up, you need to be at work at eight-thirty. I don't know what eight-thirty is, and I don't understand what late is or why you get so grouchy about it.

You yell "Hurry up, pokey." I am not pokey! And I am not a grown-up, I am three. I am moving at the normal speed for a three-year-old. When I get dressed I work hard to get the buttons buttoned and to get the heel of the sock in the right place. I chew my toast and sip my juice. You must not chew, you eat so fast. On my way to brush my teeth the dog brings me his ball and I throw it and then I go to my jewel drawer to pick out two or three necklaces to wear. I don't mean to be slow, it's just I find so many things to do.

YOU YELL A LOT IN THE MORNING. IT MAKES ME
FEEL BAD. IT WOULD BE BETTER IF WE WOULD:

Slow down!

It takes me a while to wake up, I need to cuddle with my bear under the covers, and then once my eyes are ready to stay open, I take a big stretch. I like it when you sit on the bed next to me when I'm waking up. Then I'm ready to roll out of bed and get ready for the day. Please plan enough time in the morning for me to wake up, dress at my pace, and eat my breakfast. And make sure you have enough time to sit down and chew your breakfast. It's good for you!

Develop a routine.

Some mornings you have me get my clothes on right when I get out of bed and other mornings I get dressed after breakfast. Yesterday you let me watch *Sesame Street* but today you said no. Every morning is different, I don't know what is going to happen next. It would be a lot easier for me if we did the same thing every day in the same order. You could tell me that our get-up-and-go routine has five steps, one for each finger on my hand. First we cuddle, second I put my clothes on, third eat breakfast, fourth brush teeth, and fifth go out to the car. I will need your help remembering the order at first, but soon I will be reminding you what comes next. Please don't yell at me if I get distracted by my necklaces or the dog, loud voices make it even harder for me to stay on task. I prefer to hear "Good for you, you are all dressed and ready for breakfast." On days we don't have to get up and go you can tell me it is a lazy day and we can have a special lazy routine.

Make choices the night before.

I like to decide what I'm going to wear, what I want for breakfast, and which toy is going to ride with me in the car. You seem to be in too much of a hurry for my decisions in the morning. Help me choose what clothes I'll wear before I go to bed, we could set them on my chair where I will see them when I wake up. Before we go up for nighttime teeth brushing I could help set my place for breakfast and pack my bag for day care. It would help if you make your choices and get organized before you go to bed, too. It's hard for me to stay on task when you are running around the house looking for your keys or ironing a shirt.

Naps

*You want me to take a long nap, go to bed
early, and then sleep late in the morning.
I just don't need that much sleep.*

Look at me! I'm pouring my own juice and I can
put the peanut butter on my toast. I can do lots of
things that a baby and even a two-year-old can't
do. I am changing and my need for sleep is changing, too. When I was a baby I needed lots of sleep
and when I was two I just didn't have enough energy to make it through the day without a nap.
Now that I'm three I don't always need a nap. I

must get all the sleep I need at night because when nap time comes my body just doesn't go to sleep. If I do take a nap then I have trouble getting to sleep at nighttime. Grown-ups seem to need a lot of sleep, maybe when I'm a grown-up I'll start taking naps again.

YOU INSIST I TAKE A NAP, I REFUSE. HERE'S HOW TO WORK WITH ME ON THIS:

Change nap time to rest time.

You can get me to bed but you can't force me to sleep. Tell me that you know that some days my body has had enough sleep and that I don't need a nap. Now that I am three we are going to have a rest time every day, no more nap time. Rest time will start with a story and then I can choose to listen to a music tape, a story tape, or look at books. If I feel like sleeping I can. If I do fall asleep, please don't let me sleep more than an hour. Rest time will last for one hour. I can help you set the timer. When it goes off I will know that rest time is over.

Be sure that you rest during rest time, too. You get really grumpy when you haven't had a rest.

NEGOTIATIONS

I am trying to learn about give-and-take.
But you want me to do all the giving and
you are doing all the taking!

You want to leave the park. No, I want to swing. No, it's time to go now, we need to get dinner started. But Mom, I have been waiting to swing and now it's my turn. It seems to you that lately I never take no for an answer, that I'm always trying to negotiate. You're right. When I was two I would just say no. At times I got so frustrated with always being told what to do that I just lay on the floor and screamed. Now I understand that you need to leave the park. But couldn't you stop and listen to what I need? I need a chance to swing.

PLEASE LISTEN AND CONSIDER MY REQUESTS.
I AM A PERSON, TOO. I WOULD LIKE IT
IF YOU WOULD:

> Not discourage but encourage my
> developing social skills.

Do we have to go this minute? Would five extra minutes at the park really make a difference in dinner? Taking five extra minutes can make a difference for me. If we leave right now you get what you want, you win and I lose. If you say, "Okay, before we leave I will give you ten big pushes on the swing and then you can help me set the table for dinner," we both win. That feels much better to me.

You are concerned that if you listen to me I will not learn to respect authority. You would like me to just do what you say, to be obedient. But how does being obedient prepare me for the future? Does it help me think about what is best for me, to solve problems and to stand up for what I need? How will I be able to protect myself from bad guys if I'm not allowed to question authority?

Let me win, a lot.

Give me lots of opportunities to negotiate. "Do you want to get out of the bath now or in five minutes?" Ten minutes! "Okay, if you stay in for ten minutes then we will only have time for two stories. Lights go out at eight-thirty. What have you decided, to get out now, in five minutes, or in ten minutes?" It may seem like you are always giving in, but think of it as a step in teaching me to work with others. The more experience I have at negotiating the more likely I will be able to come up with alternatives when I am playing with my friends. Before I could negotiate I would grab the blocks I wanted away from my friend Sean. Now I can think about what he might want and suggest a trade. Maybe if I give him this round block he will let me have that flat one.

Set firm limits.

I will need you to teach me when things are not negotiable. No is easier for me to accept when you tell me why. I need to hear "It is never okay to cross the street without a grown-up, this is not negotiable. People in cars can't always see children or stop fast enough when they do. We have this important rule to keep you safe."

NIGHTMARES

Nooooo, I won't go in the water, the snakes will get me!

When we went to the zoo, we saw lots of snakes. On the way home in the car, Kevin threw something at me and said "It's a snake, watch out, it might get you." Snakes scare me, I don't understand them. Kevin said that a snakebite can kill people. Lots of things scare me, big dogs, loud trucks, and monsters. Last night when I was asleep I saw a big yellow snake coming after me. I got so scared I woke up and screamed. Even though I was awake and you were holding me I could still see the snake. I was so afraid.

I NEED YOUR HELP, I CAN'T FIGHT THE BAD DREAMS ON MY OWN. HERE'S WHAT I NEED YOU TO DO:

Come fast, be calm, and stay as long as I need you.

When you hear me scream please come fast. It doesn't start to get better until you are there. Then hold me and say "It's okay, I'm with you now." You are so big and strong I'm sure you can fight off the snake. I know you want to go back to your bed, but I need you, so please stay with me until I go back to sleep. It might help if I had a drink of water, went to the bathroom, or listened to my favorite bedtime music. My body wants to go back to sleep, I just need a little help.

Respect my fears.

It's lunchtime and I can still see that snake. I'm still scared. I'm not sure I can go to sleep tonight. I am afraid the snake will come back again in my sleep. Don't tell me it was only a dream, it was real to me. When you listen, really listen to me talk about my dream, I feel better. I like the story about how you used to have dreams when you were little and how your mother taught you to change the end of the dream so it wasn't so scary. I could change my snake dream. I would have a special snake whistle that made snakes disappear when I blow it.

Play with me. Read to me.

My friend Matthew and I have been pretending there are monsters in the backyard. We are the all-powerful superkids who can run faster than any monsters. The monsters just can't get us. Pretending about scary things during the day makes them not so scary at night. I like it when you pretend with me, too. Let me decide what we are going to do. I want you to be a monster, not a mean monster, but a nice monster. We will be friends like in the story you read to me about the monster in the closet. I like that story. Can we read it again?

Make my room friendly.

Things are much scarier at night when it is dark. I would feel safer if you would leave a night-light on and leave the door open. Matthew has a dream catcher that hangs over his bed. It catches bad dreams. He made it at school. I want one to catch my bad dreams. Please sit with me in my room with the light out. Together we can look for scary shadows, and make it better.

Encourage sweet dreams.

I like to watch TV but some of the shows that Kevin watches at night are scary. It is easier to go to sleep when I have happy thoughts in my head. And it's easier to go to sleep when you are relaxed and spend time with me before saying good night. Good night and sweet dreams to you, too.

NIGHTTIME DRYNESS

*I wear big boy pants all day because
I use the potty. At bedtime I wear a
diaper. I guess I'm not ready to be a big
boy at night.*

Cowboy underpants are the best. They aren't big
and lumpy like diapers. One time I wore cowboy
underpants to bed. You said I was a big boy now
and didn't need diapers anymore. But I woke up
because I was all wet from pee. I could tell you
were mad, when you said "Taylor, why didn't you
get up and use the potty?" I'm sorry, I didn't mean
to be a bad boy. I didn't know the pee was coming
until it was too late. How will I know how to keep
the pee from coming at night?

I WANT TO BE A BIG BOY AT NIGHTTIME, TOO!
IT WOULD HELP IF YOU WOULD:

Mellow out.

My being dry seems very important to you. You
get so excited when I'm dry and angry when I'm
not. I like to make you happy, and I'm doing well
during the day, but I don't seem to have control of

the pee at night. Maybe if I didn't close my eyes and go to sleep I would be able to stay dry. I need your help in learning to use the potty, but all the excitement and yelling that goes with it makes it harder. When you are under control it helps me be relaxed and do a better job.

Let's wait, I can try again later.

I want to be dry at night. Why won't my body cooperate? Maybe it's because I'm such a good sleeper, I just can't tell when I need to pee. My body just doesn't seem to be ready to hold the pee all night long. I think this might be like learning to walk, you can't do it then you can. Even though I don't like wearing a diaper it's better than waking up all wet. Once I wake up dry for three days in a row, then I might be ready to wear my cowboy underpants to bed again.

While I'm waiting for my body to be ready to hold the pee you can teach me some good nighttime habits. Tell me that I can't have any cola or chocolate milk after dinner, they make it harder to stay dry. I will have only a few sips of water at bedtime. And instead of just going to the potty right before I get in bed I can start going a half hour before bedtime and then again at bedtime. That way I'll get all the pee out. I don't know how long it will be before I can be a big boy at night, but I hope it's soon! You probably hope so, too.

Night Waking

You have always helped me go to sleep, and now you expect me to do it on my own. I want to sleep in your bed!

Mooom, I'm awake and want to cuddle in your nice warm bed. Some nights I have scary dreams that wake me up and I really need you to comfort me. But most of the time I just wake up and I don't know how to get back to sleep. When I was a baby I fell asleep in your arms. If I woke up at night you held me close and we rocked together until I went back to sleep. Every night since I've been in my big-girl bed you have lain next to me until I fall asleep. It's easy to get to sleep all cuddled up next to you.

You say I have turned into a thrasher, rolling all over the bed. I don't want to be a thrasher. You want me to stay in my own bed, but I don't know how to get back to sleep. My body is used to going to sleep listening to your breathing, feeling your warmth. I don't know how to go to sleep without you.

I WILL NOT BE ABLE TO STAY IN MY BED ALL NIGHT WITHOUT YOUR HELP. I NEED YOU TO:

Teach me to fall asleep without you.

Explain to me that you are not going to lie with me at bedtime anymore, it makes it hard for you to get a good night's sleep. You will still read to me and give me my back rub. Then you will give me three kisses and three hugs and leave. Promise you will come back and check on me in five minutes, I get anxious when I'm alone in the dark. Ask me what I think will help me get to sleep. Maybe cuddling with my teddy bear makes it easier. Or I could listen to a sleepy-time music tape.

I really liked it when you lay with me, learning how to fall asleep on my own is not going to be easy. I will probably beg you to lie with me. When you leave I might scream or get up and follow you.

Change is hard, I don't like it. If you really, really want me to learn to sleep on my own you will have to stick to your plan. If you lie down with me after I scream long enough, I will learn that all I have to do is scream to get you back in my room. So when I test to see if you really mean it, you are going to have to remind me that it is bedtime, and I am supposed to be in my bed. I might need you to take me back to bed. Please don't start to yell, just take me back and tell me you will be back in five minutes. You may have to do this a lot the first night. My desire to have the old way has to find out how determined you are to make the change. Once I realize this is the way it's going to be, then I will start to learn how to get to sleep.

> Encourage but don't force me back in my
> bed in the middle of the night.

Once I learn to go to sleep on my own it will be easier for me to go back to sleep when I wake in the middle of the night. Let me know that if I need to come into your room I can, you will leave a sleeping bag by the bed. I can be near you in my sleeping bag and that way everyone has a sleeping space and can get a good night's sleep. Even after I have learned to go to sleep on my own there will be nights when I need you close. I'm trying hard to be a big kid, but it's hard some days.

OBSESSIONS

I am a boy who loves trains, the color pink,
and the letter W.

Look, Mom, the letter *W*, and I see it again over there. You don't seem to like the letter *W*. Whenever I point it out you say "Yes, honey, I see it" in a tired voice. Oh hooray! They have pink sandals. Look, Mom, pink sandals. I have to have the pink sandals. No, the blue sandals are not okay. I want the pink sandals! This is really important to me, pink is my favorite color. Do you have a favorite color? Isn't that how favorites work?

HERE ARE SOME WAYS TO WORK WITH
ME ON THIS:

Patience, please.

When I was a baby I didn't know that I was separate from you. You made all the decisions about what colors and clothing I wore, how my hair looked, and what toys I played with. But now I am three, I am seeing and learning so many things. Having favorites is one way I organize all the things around me. I can't take in everything I see and hear, so I choose my favorites and I spend my time on those things. My most favorite things are a part of me. When I have them around me I feel good.

Pacifiers

When I was a baby you gave me a pacifier when I cried. It helped me feel better. It still does! Now you want to take it away.

My pacifier and I are good friends. You say I am a big boy now, I don't need a pacifier. I am big, I can do a lot of things a baby can't do, like dress myself, use the potty, and ride a tricycle. But being big can be hard sometimes, like when the puzzle pieces won't go in right or my blocks fall over or when Kevin and his friends won't let me play with them. What will I do if I don't have my pacifier? How will I get rid of the icky feelings?

CHANGE IS HARD. I CAN PROBABLY GIVE UP
MY PACIFIER BUT IT WON'T BE EASY. I WILL
NEED YOU TO:

Let me help decide how to stop using my pacifier.

Tell me that one of the things I need to do now that I am three is to stop using my pacifier. Have the dentist tell me why I need to quit using it. Then talk with me about the different ways I could stop. I could just decide to stop, or I could do it gradually. For one week I could use it only when I was at home, the next week only at rest time and bedtime, and the third week (three weeks because I am three) only at bedtime. After that no more pacifier. We could make a chart showing the three weeks and put stars up after every day.

It would help if I could decide how to get rid of my pacifiers. We could put them in a box and send them to my new baby cousin, or I could give them to my neighbor, whose new baby grandson has a sick heart. I want my pacifiers to have a good home.

Give me lots of comfort.

I will have to learn new ways to feel better when I am upset. This is hard, I've always had my pacifier, and it worked. I need you to hold me, to rock with me, to read me a story. Distract me by showing me things that are new or different. Make sure that I don't get too hungry or tired, that's when it's the hardest to feel good. Give me my stuffed bear at rest time to cuddle with and sit by my bed. I can learn new ways, but learning takes time. Please be extra patient, I am trying. Other children may have given away their pacifiers long ago. I will, too, soon.

PARENT PREFERENCE

Go away! I love Daddy. We don't need you!

Daddy and I are playing house. I am the mommy and he is the daddy. We are going out to dinner and then we are going to dance.

You get sad when I send you away. You wonder if you did something wrong. I am not trying to hurt your feelings, it's just that I am learning about what it means to be a girl. From watching you I have learned that a girl has one special man that she spends time with. Mommies and daddies love each other, take care of each other, and spend time together. I want to be like you. When I grow up I am going to marry Daddy.

I DON'T WANT YOU TO READ TO ME, I WANT MY DADDY! HERE'S HOW TO WORK WITH ME ON THIS:

Let me spend time with Daddy!

A girl needs to spend time with her daddy. He is so special. When I was a baby I always wanted you to comfort me, you knew just the right way, and I didn't know Daddy as well. But now is my time to get to know my daddy. I love it when Daddy plays with me, he lets me put silly hats on him and then we laugh. Right now I want Daddy to wash my hair, to brush my teeth, and to fix my ouchies.

Patience, please!

I feel strongly about my time with Daddy and don't have polite words to express it, so I say "Get out of here!" or "I hate you" or "I don't want you." Please remember that I am just learning words and that I am telling you what I want in the only ways I know how. I want Daddy, and what I need from you is understanding and patience. If Daddy is on the phone and can't brush my teeth, in a calm voice tell me, and then ask me if I want to use my pink or my yellow toothbrush. It must be hard to be patient with me when I'm rejecting you, but when I'm upset, yelling doesn't help.

Daddy must be the best man in the world, you married him. I want to marry him, too. Daddy can help me learn about relationships by saying "While we're playing house you can be the mommy and I can be the daddy. But I am Mommy's husband in real life. In real life I'm the daddy, she's the mommy, and you are our special daughter."

Make room for Mommy.

Go away!" doesn't mean go away forever. Girls need their mommies. While I prefer to play and do things with Daddy, I can do some things with you. I remember you used to give me a noisy hug after my bath, I would like it if you asked me if I wanted a noisy hug. I might say no at first, but I do like those hugs. Maybe just this once. Oh yeah, there are other special things that you and I do, I forgot, I was so stuck on Daddy.

Parents' Disagreements

Pleeease, Mom, Dad always lets me.

You say the rule is no jumping on the bed, but Dad says it's okay. Dad says I can't get a cookie at the grocery store. You always let me have a cookie. I'm confused. How am I supposed to follow the rules if I don't know what they are? You say I can watch TV, and then Dad comes in and turns it off. When I fuss, he puts me in time-out. He's so mean. I want to be a good boy, you two are making it really hard for me.

YOU TWO DON'T ALWAYS AGREE ON WHAT I CAN DO. IT WOULD HELP IF YOU WOULD:

Decide on the rules.

I need to know what I can do. Please agree on most things, it is really hard for me to remember different rules for each parent. I need to hear that you two have decided on our family's rules. Tell me that some things will be different because you each like different things. Mom thinks getting a cookie is a fun treat at the grocery store because she used to do that with her mom. Dad thinks it's a treat to share his Popsicle.

Kiss and make up.

I'm sorry I made you angry. Please don't yell at each other. Your loud voices scare me. I'm not sure what I did but it must have been bad. Help me understand that sometimes you get angry because you have different ideas. People can get angry and still love each other. Right now you are going to take some time to calm down and then you will find a way to solve your differences. Please solve your problem soon. I feel all upset inside, and I can't get it to go away. Dad, I think if you kissed Mommy I would feel better.

Persistence

Why won't you listen? When I try to tell you what I want, or what I don't like, you just say I am being stubborn.

I am not stubborn! It's just that some things are important to me. I want to brush my teeth myself. I want to pour my own gravy. I want to ride my trike without my helmet. I don't like suntan lotion. And I won't take that medicine. You want me to do everything you ask your way. I am not you! When you try to force suntan lotion on me I scream. I get so frustrated and angry.

IT WOULD HELP IF YOU WOULD:

Think before you say no!

You think I say no a lot, but listen to you. No, you cannot pour the gravy. No, you can't look at my jewelry. No, you can't wear your dress-up clothes to the grocery store. No, no, no, you say it so fast. Do you really think about what I asked? You think these things are not very important, not worth the fuss, but they are important to me! Why can't I pour the gravy? What is the worst thing that could happen? How will I learn to do things for myself if you won't let me? Please save your nos for the things that are really important, like keeping me safe. I like yes, don't you?

Listen and try to understand!

You say I have to have suntan lotion on before I go outside. I want to go outside, it's just that the lotion is yucky. It would really help if you would say "Is there something about this lotion that bothers you?" Your question will help me to think about why I feel so strongly about lotion. The problem is the lotion smells bad and it stings when it gets into my eyes. Now that we both understand the problem we can talk about some solutions. If you help me learn to see problems I can become a good problem solver. With your help I can learn to use my ability to stick-to-it as an asset.

Tell me why.

If you have to say no, it helps if I know why. I need to hear "The rule in our house is that we wear a helmet when we ride trikes and bikes. The helmet protects your head in case you fall. Both Mommy and Daddy wear their helmets, too, when they ride."

PERSONAL SAFETY

Mommy, stop talking to that lady.
She is a stranger!

You told me never to talk to strangers. You said strangers are people we do not know. Strangers are bad, they do bad things. Why are you talking to that stranger?

I'm confused. How will I know who is a stranger and who is not? If a person knows my name, then are they my friend? Is the lady at the grocery store with the nice smile a stranger? Is the man at the cleaners a stranger? He always says hi and gives me a piece of candy. When does a person stop being a stranger?

We need to talk more about safety. This stranger rule is too confusing for me. I need safety rules I can understand.

I NEED YOU TO:

Teach me the reporting rule.

Tell me I must always come and check with the grown-up in charge before I go anywhere with any-body. Tell me it is the responsibility of the grown-up in charge to decide what is okay for me to do. Grown-ups always need to know where I am. Remind me that when we are at the park together you are the grown-up in charge and that when I go with our neighbor Ingela to the park she is in charge. When I am at preschool the teachers are in charge. You will tell me who is in charge, so you better make good choices. If you tell me they're okay, they're okay.

It is all right for me to have a candy at the cleaners because you are there and the man always asks you if it's okay first. Good, I always like to go to the cleaners. Ask me if I would take candy or a toy from a man who stopped his car in front of our house. No, I wouldn't, I would come and ask you first. That is the rule. Tell me that most people are friendly, but that there are a few who could harm me. It is important for me always to follow the rule, and that way I will be safe.

Tell me what to do if I get lost.

Most of the time we stay together when we are out. What will I do if I can't find you? If I am not supposed to talk to a stranger, who will help me? Tell me that if I ever get lost you want me to remember that you or whoever I came with will be looking for me. I am not to leave the store or go looking for you. I should stay put where I can be seen. I should look for a worker. In a store workers are usually around the counter and they wear a name tag. Sometimes workers wear uniforms. I should tell a worker that I am lost. I should also tell the worker my name and the name of the person I am with, but I should leave the store only with you or the grown-up with whom I came. The worker will call someone who can put their voice over a loudspeaker so everyone can hear. You will hear it and know where to come to find me. If I don't see a worker, I should talk to a mother with little children. I should tell her I am lost and ask her to get a worker. I should tell her I'm not to go anywhere with strangers. The grown-ups will work to get us together.

Teach me about keeping my body safe.

Sometimes I like to cuddle but sometimes I don't. Peter always wants to give me a hug and a kiss when he leaves, but I don't like it, it doesn't feel good. Couldn't I just wave good-bye? Please let me decide what is right for my body. Talk to me about good touches, like hugs and kisses, bad touches, like a hit or a kick, and uncomfortable touches, which just don't feel right. Tell me that my body belongs to me and that I can refuse any kind of touch from anyone, even you. When you tell me that I can say no I feel safe.

I need to know the rules about my special body parts. These are the parts of my body that are covered by a swimming suit. These private body parts are special and only I have the right to touch them. There may be a time when a parent or doctor might need to touch them, but you will tell me and explain why first. If someone asks to see my private parts I should say no. I should say no and then go and tell you or another grown-up. I am not to let other people touch my private parts and I should not touch theirs. People are less likely to harm children who say no and are strong. Tell me that you will do your best to help me keep my body safe, but that I am to tell you if anyone touches me in ways that make me uncomfortable. Tell me that touching secrets are bad secrets and that in our family we always tell about touching.

Playing alone

Mommy, will you play with me?

We spend a lot of time together. You help me get dressed, fix me breakfast, brush my hair, and we run errands together. But then you say you have things to do and tell me to go play. I want to play with you. Playing isn't the same as getting dressed, playing with you feels good. It makes me happy. You wish I would just go and play by myself. You say "Look at all those toys, go find something to play with." But, Mom, some things I just can't do without you. I need your help with the zoo puzzle, and I can't get the dolls dressed by myself. When you play you show me new ways to shape the Play-Doh and teach me new words. Today what I really want you to do is play pretend with me. I will be the princess and you will be the stepmother. In the story we read the stepmother was mean, but you will be a nice stepmother, okay? When I pretend I explore new ideas and scary feelings, and it really helps when you do it with me.

*I NEED YOU TO PLAY WITH ME. YOU NEED TIME
FOR OTHER THINGS. SOME WAYS TO WORK WITH
ME ON THIS INCLUDE:*

Have a set playtime.

I will beg, whine, and plead until you play with me. You say not now, then when? If I could count on you to play with me every day after breakfast then I won't have to ask over and over again. Please do what I want to do first, then I will be able to play by myself or do what you want to do. Tell me that you will play with me for twenty minutes and that the buzzer will tell us when the time is over. Then you will be cleaning the kitchen.

Let's do things we both like.

I know you get tired of playing pretend when you say "I am your mom now, and you are Jennifer. No more stepmother today." Although pretending is my favorite thing to do right now, there are other things I like to do with you. We could dig in the garden, vacuum the sofa and look for hidden treasure, or make some cookies. What would you like to do? I really just want to be with you.

Give me some ideas.

I liked it when you said "What if you put some blankets over this table and made a home for your stuffed animals?" Most of the time you just say "Go play, I have work to do." I see all my toys and I don't quite know what to do. If you can't play with me please help me get started and then stay near. I might need your help.

PRESCHOOL (SELECTION OF)

You say three-year-olds are old enough to go to preschool. Do preschools know that I like to play with trucks? Are there trucks at preschool?

I am not good at sitting still. Will I have to sit at a table at preschool? My friend Ryan goes to school. Can I go to Ryan's school? He has a big picture he said he painted at school on his refrigerator. Will I get to paint a picture with yellow and red—my favorite colors? Do the teachers at preschool smile a lot? I like people who smile a lot. People who frown scare me. I think preschool could be a good thing. I like to play with other children. It will be fun, won't it?

PLEASE PICK A FUN PRESCHOOL. THE THINGS THAT ARE IMPORTANT TO ME ARE:

Lots of free play.

I don't need to sit at a table and listen to a teacher to learn. The best way for me to learn is to play. When I build a tower with blocks I am learning about shapes and balance. In the sandbox I learn that it takes more sand to fill the big cup than the little cup. In the dress-up area I can pretend to be Daddy, or a firefighter, or a cook. When I do finger painting I see what happens when colors get mixed together. All I need in order to learn is plenty of time, space, and lots of fun things to play with. Having a grown-up around to make suggestions like "What do you think would happen if you added green?" helps, too. Learning is fun, isn't it?

A nice teacher.

Please pick a teacher who likes energetic three-year-olds. For me to be comfortable at school I need to feel good about the teacher. I like people who get a big smile on their face when they see me and give me a big hello. Make sure that the teacher doesn't just talk to children but also listens. I like it when a grown-up gets right down where she can hear me. Ask her what she would do if a boy took a toy away from me. I don't like that, and sometimes I get so angry I bite when it happens. Maybe she can help me learn to say "No, my toy."

PRETEND

We are pretending we're kitties.

Amanda is a yellow kitty and I am a black and white kitty. Would you like to pet us? Kitties like to be petted gently on the head. Meow, meow, this little kitty is hungry for some milk and cookies. Would you be the nice person who found the kittens? Do you have a snack for the kittens? The kittens would like to go outside and play. Can the kittens play in the backyard?

It's fun to be a kitten. Kittens are soft and playful and people like them. I also like to be a mommy, a daddy, a princess, a horse, and a firefighter. When I pretend I can feel what it's like to be someone or something else. Sometimes I pretend about things that scare me. After I went to the fire station in preschool I pretended there was a fire and that I saved all the people and animals. I fought that fire over and over again. At first it was really scary, but each time I felt more powerful, more able to get everyone out of the fire before they got hurt.

PRETENDING IS AN IMPORTANT WAY I LEARN
ABOUT THE THINGS AROUND ME. YOU
CAN HELP BY:

Pretending with me.

Would you play Momma and baby with me? Please don't say it's bedtime. Just play with me for a few minutes. I'll be the mommy and you're the baby. Look what Momma has for you, some cookies. Here, eat them up. Now it is bedtime. Lie down right here and Momma will sit with you. It's okay, baby, I'll stay with you as long as you need me. I won't let any scary dreams hurt you. Good night, sweetie. I like being the momma, giving you treats, and helping you feel safe. Thanks for pretending with me, now I think I can go to sleep.

Letting me be in charge.

Don't tell Amanda and me that kittens don't eat cookies. This is Amanda and my story, not yours.

These are special kittens, pretend kittens, and in pretend all kinds of things are possible. We will let you know when and how we want your help. Now could you please get these kittens a snack?

Giving me some props.

Amanda and I are pretending we are going to a party. Will you let us wear some of your lipstick? I am going to wear my pink necklace and Amanda is wearing my white one. Could we wear some of your shoes? That would help us feel like very fancy ladies. And could you turn on some dancing music? It's really fun to dress up. At day care there are hats, scarves, clothes, and shoes to use for dress-up. They even have pretend food. Maybe you have some things that you could put in a box for me. Then I would have my own dress-up box. That would really be good.

PUNISHMENT

You always want me to do what you want.

Get your clothes on! Quit playing with your straw! No hitting! Don't interrupt, I'm on the phone! Sit still! When I don't obey, you get angry. Then you yell at me, hit me, or put me in my room. It scares me when you get angry. I don't want to make you angry. It's just that I can't always obey.

WHAT I REALLY NEED IS FOR YOU TO:

> Don't just say no, teach me what
> I need to know.

You say don't interrupt. But, Mom, I need to tell you something. Kevin needs to use the potty and he can't get his pants unsnapped. This is important. How would you like me to get your attention? You need to talk with me about interrupting. Tell me that if you are talking to another person, in person or on the phone, I need to wait until you stop. I can let you know that I need to talk to you by holding your hand. If it's an emergency, like Kevin's stuck pants or someone getting hurt, I can wave my arms over my head, and you will stop right away. Is it an emergency if I want a cookie or if I need you to get the Play-Doh out? There are a lot of things that I need to learn and I need you to teach me.

Help me be successful.

Before we go shopping or out to eat it helps if you tell me what is going to happen and how I need to behave. I will try to do what you want. But please don't ask me to do things that I just can't do. I am not a grown-up and I can't sit still for a long time waiting for food to come. It would help if I had something to do. Could we bring some crayons and paper for me to color on? And I have trouble getting my clothes and my shoes on in the morning. I go to my room but then I see my toys. I'm sorry, I just forget. Does that ever happen to you? Can you help me find a way to get dressed without getting distracted?

Focus on solutions, not punishment.

Oh, my juice spilled. Please, please don't spank me. It hurts, and I get all upset inside. You think a spanking will help me remember the rule about not playing with the straw. You're wrong. I'm not thinking about the juice, I'm thinking about how mean you are. Instead of a spanking show me the mess that I've made. Then give me a rag and help me clean it up. If you can without yelling, remind me of the rule about straws and ask me why I think we have that rule. Wow, juice really does make a mess. I better be more careful with my straw next time.

Rules

No pulling the dog's tail. No cushions off the sofa. No crossing the street without a grown-up. No cookies before dinner. All day long, no! no! no!

I don't like rules. Why do you have to have so many rules? It seems like I'm always getting put in time-out for breaking a rule. I don't mean to make you angry, it's just that when I'm busy building a house for my doll and she needs a soft bed I don't remember the no-cushions-off-the-sofa rule.

What is a rule anyway? You say the rule is no cushions off the sofa. But when my friend Sean was over we built a fort and used the sofa cushions. You didn't get angry, and I didn't have to go to time-out. Does the rule change from day to day? How will I know if today I will get in trouble about cushions or if you will just frown and not say anything? It would be a lot easier if you would decide what the rule is and have it be the same every day.

I'M NOT SO SURE WHAT RULES ARE.
I NEED YOU TO:

Explain why you have rules.

I need you to tell me that rules tell us what is okay and what is not okay. Our family has rules that help to keep us safe, like the rule about not crossing the street without a grown-up and the rule that I always have to be buckled in my car seat when the car is moving. Other rules protect other people, animals, and things like toys, the sofa and Mommy's music box. We have a rule about pulling the dog's tail because that hurts the dog, and hurting others is not okay. Why do we have a rule about no cookies before dinner? That doesn't hurt the dog and it doesn't hurt me.

Explain that rules are not just for three-year-olds but for everyone. Show me that you have a special belt in the car that you wear in the car to keep you safe. Tell me that before you could drive a car you had to know the rules of driving. When we come to a red light tell me that the rule says that you must stop until the light turns green. If you don't stop, then you might run into another car, and people and cars would get hurt.

Not make too many rules.

Three-year-olds need to be able to move, explore, and create. There are so many rules at Aunt Sara's house that if I leave your side I get in trouble. Aunt Sara always has a frown on her face when I'm at her house. I'm not a bad girl, I am only three. Let's not go there.

Don't just tell me what not to do, tell me what to do!

I pull Perky's tail because I want to play with her. You tell me the rule is no pulling on the dog's tail. Okay, but what can I do? Tell me that if I want to play with Perky I can throw her ball. Then show me how and where to throw the ball. Let's play with Perky together.

Be patient, please.

I have a hard time following rules. Sometimes I just forget, other times I'm not sure if today you have the same rule as before, so I have to test it. When I was at Grandma's house I had a cookie even though I knew the rule about no cookies before dinner. It was a chocolate chip cookie, my favorite kind, and I just couldn't be in that room without having one or two. It helps when you remind me of the crossing-the-street rule while we are putting our coats on to go outside. If you see me starting to grab Perky's tail ask me, "What is the rule about playing with Perky?" When I tell you the rule is no pulling Perky's tail, that helps me remember. Please don't yell when I break a rule, I get so upset by your anger that I forget what caused it. If I run into the street to get my ball, remind me that it is not safe for children to be in the street without an adult. People in cars can't always see children because children are small. Tell me that if I go into the street again we will have to go inside and play. Rules are so hard to remember and there are so many of them, are you sure they are all necessary?

SEPARATION

I want you to stay and play with me!

You are excited about preschool. I'm not so sure. I've never been in a place like this before. There is a kitchen with pretend food and dress-up clothes, a train, a big sandbox, blocks, and a big climbing toy. The tables and chairs are just my size, and there's a low water fountain, too. You say "Now be a big boy and go play. Mommy will be back in a little while." No! I am staying with you. I want you to come over to the train with me. That way if someone grabs my train, or pushes me, you will be there to help me. With you nearby I feel safe. I need you. I don't think I can stay here without you. Don't go, Mommy!

I AM AFRAID AND I NEED YOUR HELP.
I NEED YOU TO:

Help me feel safe.

Please don't leave me the first day. Show me where we sign in, where my cubbie is, and take me to the bathroom. On the way home talk with me about what we did at preschool. Ask me, "What do you want to play with next time?" Tell me that when you are not there the teachers are there if I need them. If I need to go to the potty, I am to tell a teacher, and one of them will go with me. Then remind me of the teachers' names. There are so many new things, it will take me a while to learn them all.

Create a good-bye ritual.

It is hard for me to say good-bye because I don't feel good when you leave. If you really can't stay with me, help me get my things in my cubbie, say hello to the teacher, walk around the room with me so I can get an idea of what I want to do, and then say good-bye. Give me a really big bear hug and tell me you will be back right after snack and then go. I will probably be crying, the moment you leave is the saddest. Once you're gone I will find a way to start feeling better, the teacher might help. It might take a while but saying good-bye will get easier.

Plan time for cuddling.

Please don't run errands after school, I want to go home. Trying new things makes me tired and cranky. At school I am learning to be more independent, but when I get home I just want to cuddle. Thanks!

Sexual Curiosity

*Why does Mommy have breasts and you
don't? Will our new baby have a penis?
Where do babies come from?*

I know that I am a boy, you have been using that
word when you talk to me for a long time. You tell
me to be a good boy when you leave me at day care
and to act like a big boy when I want to be carried.
But I'm not sure what being a boy means. When I
was two I noticed that my body was different from
Mom's or my friend Sara's, I am more like you, I
have a penis. Being a boy has something to do with
having a penis. If you and I are boys why don't I
have hair down there? Why isn't my penis as big
as yours?

143

It's not so easy understanding all this body stuff. I have lots of questions. Why do you act so quiet and funny when I ask you about being a boy? I'm trying to understand all the things around me. You don't have problems when I ask questions about the clouds, the stars, and the moon. When you don't know the answer, you just say "I'm not sure, let's go to the library and find a book to help us answer that question." I depend on you to help me understand myself and the world around me.

I NEED YOUR HELP TO LEARN ABOUT WHAT BEING A BOY OR A GIRL IS ALL ABOUT. I NEED YOU TO:

Answer all my questions!

Please don't tell me I'm too young to understand. I am aware of the difference now and I want to know. If you won't answer my questions I will find other ways to get the answers or I will come up with my own ideas. Instead of understanding that boys and girls were born with a few different but very special body parts, I might think that girls' penises fell off when they were born. I will hope that my penis won't fall off. If it does then I will have to start being a girl. I will learn that you are not a good source of information, at least when it comes to bodies. It's okay if you don't know the answer, we can always get a book and learn together.

When we were at the grocery store I asked where babies come from and you told me in your very quiet voice you would tell me later. Why were you whispering? It's later now, why haven't you told me? Is there something bad or scary about babies? You told me we were going to have a new baby, where is it now? I am not too young to hear that the baby grows in a special place inside the mommy called the uterus until it is ready to be born. A book with pictures of a baby growing inside the mommy would help me understand what is happening.

Don't get angry. We were just looking!

Joshua and I are both interested in our bodies. He said he would show me his penis if I showed him mine. Why are you getting so upset? If you don't want us to examine each other's bodies, just tell us it's time to get our clothes back on. You could say "It looks like you two are checking out each other's bodies. Both of you have penises, since you both are boys." Offering us some milk and cookies will help us change activities.

I am ready to learn that the parts of my body covered by a swimming suit are called my private parts. It is all right for me to touch my private parts, but I'm not to let other people touch them. There may be times when Mom or Daddy or a doctor may need to touch my private parts, but they will always tell me what they are doing and why.

Sharing

*It's mine, and even though I
wasn't touching it when he took it I was
playing with it.*

This is my barn. I am putting all the cows in the barn and some of the chicken. I built a fence for the other animals so they won't get out. No! That is mine! I was playing with that horse. Give it back! Mom, Josh took my horse. Make him give it back. No, no, please don't tell me to share. I don't want to give it to him. If he takes it then it's not mine anymore, it's his. I don't want to give my horse away.

I DON'T UNDERSTAND WHY YOU ALWAYS WANT ME TO SHARE. IT WOULD HELP IF YOU WOULD:

> Assure me that sharing is not the
> same as giving away.

I don't know that sharing is not the same as giving something away. My toys are important to me, I do not want to give them away. Let me know that you understand that sharing is hard, that it might feel like the horse isn't mine if I let Josh play with it. Tell me that if I let Josh play with the horse it is still mine and that you will make sure that Josh leaves the horse at our house when he goes home.

Teach me how to share.

Why should I let Josh take the horse? Then I will have fewer horses! Point out that Josh came over today to play and that he might want to play farm with me. Let's see what Josh wants to do with the horse. The horse Josh has is galloping through the field, maybe one of the other horses would like to join him. Tell me that if I really want that horse I might be able to offer Josh a cow or a different horse or I could tell him I want to have a turn with the horse when he's done. Once Josh and I have made the trade, tell us "Good sharing." This sharing thing is not as easy as you think.

Let me decide what I will share.

Mommy, do you share everything? Can I wear your pretty blue necklace? Tell me that there are some things that people choose not to share. Before Josh comes over help me put away the things I am choosing not to share. Remind me that if I put them away I won't be able to play with them when Josh is over. Then help me select toys that I will share.

Shopping

No, no, please don't stop at the grocery store. I'm tired and I'm hungry and I just want to go home! I don't have enough energy for the grocery store, the dry cleaners, or the garden store.

It takes a lot of energy to sit still, look but not touch, and use my quiet voice. These things don't come natural to me, so I have to work very hard to make them happen. Sometimes I can "be good," but only for a while. The longer we shop, the harder it becomes for me to follow the rules. My body starts to feel yucky inside. I see so many things that look interesting. You get to touch things and put them in the basket, why can't I? You get all the yeses and I only get nos. "No, you can't have a cookie" and "No, we are not buying that cereal" and "No, you can't take things from the shelf." Shopping is no fun, and it is definitely not for three-year-olds.

PLEASE DON'T TAKE ME SHOPPING. IF I MUST GO YOU COULD MAKE IT BETTER BY:

Being organized.

If I am not tired or hungry a short trip to the store is okay. No long trips, being strapped into a cart for too long makes me want to scream. Please go to the store when a lot of other people aren't there. Waiting in line is hard, especially when the candy is close to my reach. Make a list, get those things, and then leave, but not before stopping to let me throw a coin into the fountain.

Let me put some things in the cart.
I want to help!

Give me a job, I'm a big kid and I can help. I can pick three bananas, two oranges, and look for the kind of crackers we like. Tell me what we are going to get next and let me take it off the shelf, or hand it to me if I can't reach it and let me put it in the cart. When I am busy helping I don't have much trouble.

Before we leave for the store tell me that you are making a shopping list and ask me what things I think you should put on it. Then if I see a candy bar while we are shopping you can remind me that we buy only the things that are on our shopping list. Make sure you include some treats on the list, I will want to hold these myself. On the way to do our shopping ask me to tell you our shopping rules. When I have them in my mind before going into the store, we don't have as many problems.

SHYNESS

I want to play with that girl but I just don't know how.

I've been watching that girl pick the little flowers from the grass and then throw them up into the air. She is laughing, running, and climbing up on the tree stumps. I would like to do that, too. How can I make friends with her? Two times she ran by me, but I didn't say anything.

I NEED YOUR HELP. HERE ARE SOME WAYS YOU CAN HELP ME WITH THIS:

Teach me what to say.

I want to say something to that girl but I don't have the words. Can you give me some words? Suggest that I say "Hi! My name is Amanda, can I play with you?" Tell me that I need to look up at her face when I talk and I should speak loud enough so that she can hear me. If I can't get her attention maybe I could pick some flowers and take them over to her. Then I can say "Would you like to throw these?"

Help me feel in control.

Being around other children is exciting and scary. At preschool some of the kids are moving all the time. I stay away from them. I don't know what they are going to do next. You and the teacher would like me to spend more time playing with the other children, but I don't feel comfortable. I stay over by the book area or by the Play-Doh where I can watch everything that is happening. I wish I had a friend in this school, someone I knew and could play with. Then I would feel braver. Could you invite Moriah over to our house? I know you are friends with Allysa's mom and have suggested she come over, but she's too wild for me. Moriah doesn't talk in a loud voice, and she likes to play dress-up. I would like to play dress-up, too.

Let's have a talk about play dates. Tell me that when Moriah arrives I should say "Hi, would you like to see my room?" and "What would you like to play?" Show me that you have crackers, cheese, and juice ready for a snack and that I can help you serve it when we're ready. Have me put any toys away that I don't want to share and help me think about toys we can play with. Let's not make this play date too long. I think two hours is long enough, any more and I might get tired and start having trouble. It's better to end playing when we're still playing well than when one or both of us are grouchy.

Prepare me for new situations.

Where are we going? Who is going to be there? What is going to happen? I like being at home where I feel comfortable, when we go to new places there are so many things and people that are, well, new. You want me to go and play with the other kids, but I'm not ready. It would help if you would tell me before we arrive what to expect. Then once we get there go with me to where the children are and stay with me. I will need to watch what the other children are doing. Help me think about what I see and talk with me about how I could play with or how I might join in with the other children. Then let me decide what I will do.

Please don't call me shy. When I hear that I feel less confident to try new things. I would rather you tell anyone who asks that I am a thinker and that I like to watch before I join in. Being a thinker is good, I think.

Sibling Fights

"Who started this?" "She did!"

I pushed her because she was too close to me and because I was angry that I got sent to time-out this morning when she took my doll and won't give it back. It was her fault I hit her. She always gets me in trouble. You like her more than me!

You say "Stop that fighting, I want to see you playing nicely together." I am supposed to love my sister. I do. Do people who love each other get along all the time? Am I just supposed to let her take my toys, call me a stinky tomato, and sit in my chair? No! I won't let that happen. You may want peace and quiet, but these things are important to me.

HERE'S HOW YOU CAN WORK WITH ME ON THIS:

Wait and listen.

I want that block!" "No, I need it!" "But you have all the big blocks!" You hear yelling and you get angry. Please don't take the blocks away. Just because we're yelling at each other doesn't mean we're fighting. If you would just leave us alone we might be able to come up with our own idea for solving the problem. Maybe Rebecca has an idea of how I could build my house. Or I might decide to play with the farm. Instead of listening for loud voices, listen for hurting. If she is hurting me, don't wait, I need your help now.

Focus on solutions, not blame.

To my way of thinking fights are never my fault, and if you punish me and not her then I'll get her back, just you wait and see. It seems like you always take her side and not mine. She makes me so mad! And I hate it when you say "Who started this?" Please show us how to solve our problems. First, have each of us tell you what happened. Be sure and make her be quiet when I'm talking. She will have her turn. Then help us focus on the problem by saying "I understand, Rebecca, you were having a tea party and you wanted two dolls to attend. Lisa, you don't want Rebecca to play with your doll." Finally, ask us for our ideas for solving the problem. I might not have any ideas at first, but Rebecca is older and she might have an idea. If it's a really hard problem you might have to give us some ideas.

Sometimes I'm so angry at Rebecca that I can't

listen or think. In that case I need to hear "You girls are too angry to solve this problem right now. Go to you rooms to cool off and come out when you are feeling calmer. Then if you still have a problem you can think of some ideas to solve it."

Sibling (New Baby)

Put him down! You're my mommy, and I don't want to share you.

I have never been very good at sharing, especially my most special things. Before the baby I didn't have to share you, I was your baby, and I had you all to myself. You read me stories, danced with me, cuddled with me when I got an ouchie, and helped me build block houses for my animals. Now all you do is hold the baby, feed the baby, and talk to the baby. I'm supposed to go play with my toys. I've never been good at playing for long times by myself, what makes you think I can do it now? I need you. I'm thirsty and I can't get a drink myself. Why won't this puzzle piece fit? I'm getting so frustrated. I need your help. Please take that baby back, I want to be your only baby.

IT WAS BETTER BEFORE THAT BABY CAME. YOU CAN HELP EASE MY TRANSITION INTO BIG SISTERHOOD BY:

Talking to me about my feelings.

Grandmom said, "Isn't it great to have a little brother? Give your brother a kiss." I don't want to kiss him, I want to bite him. Why is everyone so happy about the baby? All this baby does is eat and cry. And when he cries at night I can't sleep. Hold me and tell me that babies can be demanding. At first it can be hard on everyone. If I ever get frustrated or angry at the baby I am to let you know with my words and you will listen.

Help me be involved.

Mark and Claire came over not to see me but to see the baby. They brought a present for the baby. I stood quietly by the crib when they went into the baby's room. They didn't even look at me. I pretended to be a horse and galloped around the room, and still they didn't look. Then I put the baby's pacifier in my mouth. That got your attention but only long enough for you to yell at me and put me in my room for a time-out. Can't you see that I was asking for some attention? Mark and Claire were my friends before the baby. Mark use to play hide-and-seek with me, and I would always take Claire into my room to show her my special things. Don't they like me anymore? Please find a way for me to be involved when we have guests. I don't like having to be naughty to get some attention. Maybe I could give the tour of the baby's room. And I could show pictures of the baby and with me, the big sister.

Making sure I get my turn.

We were reading a book until he started to cry. Come back, we're not done yet. Why can't you just let him cry? Please don't just leave me. Tell me to use my finger to mark the page, that you will be back. Grandmom says babies need a lot of care. When they are hungry, they are really hungry, and don't know how to wait. I think our baby is hungry, I guess you should feed him. I am a big girl and I get to stay up when the baby is napping. Then it will be my turn to have some time with you. I think today I would like to build a fort with the table and some blankets. Grandmom also told me that when that baby gets older, he will have to wait his turn, too.

Sibling (PREPARING FOR A NEW BABY)

You have a big tummy, Mommy.

Are you sick, Mommy? Is that why you need to sit down and rest? I want you to do puzzles with me. I can tell something is happening, I'm just not sure what. I do know that it is important to you that I be a big boy. I have a new room with a big-boy bed and big-boy things. And I am to use the big-boy potty. Why are you in my baby room, Mommy? This was my baby toy. Big boys still like to play with baby toys.

I'M READY TO KNOW ABOUT THE BABY. YOU CAN HELP PREPARE ME BY:

Telling me that I am going to be a big brother.

You say you are going to have a baby. I'm not sure what you mean. Could you tell me what will be happening to me? It's easier for me to under-stand that way. My friend Joshua's mom had a baby, and he got a shirt that says "I'm the big brother." Will I get a big brother shirt, too?

161

Talking to me about babies.

Joshua's baby cries a lot. Will our baby cry? Will our baby play cars with me? Joshua got in trouble when he gave his baby a car. What's a big brother supposed to do? Could we get a book about babies? The pictures would help me understand what babies can do and what they need. I'd like to look at my baby pictures. Could you tell me the story about how I cried and cried until you showed me a picture of Mickey Mouse? I still like Mickey, and I like that story. Hold me in your arms and tell me about how you cuddled with me to help me feel welcome, and how you fed me and changed my diaper. In the beginning I needed a lot of attention because I couldn't do things for myself. Our baby will need that kind of loving attention, too. Give me a big hug and tell me you loved me when I was a baby, a toddler, and now as a three-year-old. That you will always love me.

Letting me help.

Let me help get the baby's room ready. That's a big brother's job. I know a lot about being a baby. I think our baby will like this toy. Can we buy it for him? Will our baby be a boy or a girl?

Preparing me for the birth.

When are we getting our baby? Will we all go to the hospital together? Please tell me what will happen when the baby is born. I might get scared if Daddy and you are rushing around and not paying attention to me. Reassure me that you love me and that you are excited about having two children to love.

Spoiled

I didn't spoil myself!

It started when I was little. I would want something, a cookie, another story, a toy, you would say no, at least at first. Because "no" was new to me and I didn't have many words I would get so frustrated I would cry. If I was tired or hungry I'd scream. And what I learned is that no doesn't always mean no. You must like it when I'm quiet because if I yell and scream enough you give me what I want. Now that I have words I have found that asking, begging, and pleading also get me what I want.

I don't like no, I like yes much better. Wouldn't it be easier if you just said yes first? I don't really like having to do all that fussing. I could have cookies whenever I wanted, I could go to bed when I wanted, and you would fix me pancakes whenever I felt like pancakes. I will demand what I want and I will expect it now!

I HAVE LEARNED WAYS TO GET WHAT I WANT.
IF YOU WANT ME TO ACT DIFFERENTLY
YOU WILL NEED TO:

Be in charge.

One problem is that while I know what I want, I don't know what I need. I have to rely on you for

164

that. I don't know that I need to eat healthful food and I have problems when I don't get enough sleep. I know I don't make it easy for you, but I need you to decide what is best for me even when I am screaming. It may be easier to say yes, but what will happen to me when I visit Grandma's or a friend's house? I won't know how to take no for an answer. At Grandma's I will demand another video, refuse to eat the macaroni and cheese she made me for lunch, and insist on taking home the toy lion from her toy box. I might not be invited again.

Say no and mean it!

You say no cookies before lunch, but yesterday I begged and begged and you finally gave me one. What about today, can I have a cookie today? Will you say yes if I ask three times, four times, ten times? How will I know what the limits are if they are different from day to day? Decide what the rules are going to be, tell me, and then don't change your mind. Don't be mean about it, tell me that you know how much I love cookies and that I can have a cookie for dessert. Expect that I will be frustrated and angry, it's hard to understand that I can't always get what I want. I'm three now and I can start to learn to deal with frustration, if you help me. Life will be easier for both of us when you set the limits and I follow them. But please, not too many rules to start!

STREET SMARTS

I am not a baby anymore, I am three. A three-year-old is old enough to cross the street by herself!

There are lots of things I can do, I can dress myself, brush my own teeth, get juice out of the refrigerator, and go visit my friend Sara. Why do I need you to walk with me across the street when I go to her house? Why do you get so angry when I go across the street alone? I always look both ways before I cross the street. Why are you so mad at me?

HERE IS HOW YOU CAN WORK WITH ME ON THIS:

Give me more information.

I know a lot of words and I am very interested in why things happen. Telling me not to cross the street isn't enough anymore, I need to know why. Tell me that drivers have a hard time seeing children and may not be able to stop their car in time. Tell me that being hit by a car would be a very big ouch. Put our car on the side of the street and then let me sit in the driver's seat with you. Have Sara and her mom walk in front of our car. Ask me if I can see Sara. Can I see Sara's mom? Is it easier to see them together?

Tell me that you love me very much and you never want anything bad to happen to me. That is why you are teaching me important safety rules. Safety rules are not just for kids but for everyone. Big kids and grown-ups follow safety rules, too. Show me that you want to stay safe, too, and that is why you always wear your seat belt, you stand on the sidewalk instead of the street when you talk to neighbors, and you always wear your helmet when you ride your bike. There are many safety rules, and crossing the street is part of my learning to be safe.

SUPERHEROES

I'm the pink ranger and Scott is the yellow ranger. We'll get rid of those bad guys.

I can't wait until Scott comes over so we can play Power Rangers. We like to practice our kicks and punches and make fighting sounds. Watch how I can kick. I feel so strong and brave when I'm a Power Ranger.

You say, "Not the Power Rangers again today. Why don't you two play something else?" You don't like all the fighting. But, Mom, Power Rangers fight the bad guys. Someone has to fight the bad guys. Didn't you play good guys and bad guys when you were a kid? You worry I'm learning to fight rather than to use words to solve problems. To me this is about good and bad and feeling powerful and in control. When I was two I didn't know that there were so many bad guys, but now I know, I've seen them on TV and you have warned me about them. Bad guys are really scary. Pretending lets me explore my feelings and helps me feel less scared. Scott and I play Power Rangers a lot because we get scared a lot and because it's fun.

HERE'S HOW TO WORK WITH ME ON THIS:

Set limits to my actions.

I need to be told that Power Rangers are pretend. I am not to make fighting noises to other children when I go to the park, it scares them. Remind me that the Power Rangers are the good guys and like the Power Rangers I am to be nice to other people. And I am not to kick or punch the dog, furniture, or people. If I want to practice fighting without touching anything else that is okay.

Limit my TV.

My favorite TV shows have lots of action. See that "Pow!" He really got that bad guy. After I've watched TV my body is ready to go, to practice what I saw. When I watch shows with lots of fighting that is what I learn. You can help me think about what I've seen by asking me questions about the show. You could ask "Do you think that could really happen or is it just pretend?" and "What would you do if that happened to you?" Talking about scary things with you helps me understand them. A lot of the things I see on TV scare me, maybe we should do something else.

Introduce me to real heroes.

The Power Rangers protect the world from pretend bad guys. Who protects us from the real bad guys? Tell me that police officers help protect us. Point out the police cars and show me where the police station is. I'd like to meet a real police officer, could we visit the police station? Please?

Sweets

*I love cookies. I want to have cookies
every day. I will ask and whine and cry until
I get my cookies. I make a big fuss
because it works!*

The first thing I think about in the morning is cookies. They taste so good. You say I can't have cookies for breakfast, but you don't tell me when I can have them. Making sure I get my cookies takes a lot of my time and energy, but right now they are very important to me, and when I like something, I'm not going to give up easily.

WHY DON'T WE TRY THIS:

Set a specific time when I get my
cookies every day.

If I knew that my favorite cookies would be served every day at the same time, say with lunch, I could relax and move on to other things. For a few days I might ask for cookies a couple of times before lunch. Just remind me that cookie time is lunchtime. Soon I will come to trust you that I will get my cookies at lunch and we won't have to hassle over cookies.

Make treats with me.

I love to help in the kitchen and I particularly love to taste the stuff that we bake with. When we bake I'm willing to try all different kinds of things and I am very proud to show off the wonderful things we make.

Tantrums

*My body feels all yucky and
I can't hold it in.*

You asked me "Are you ready to leave the park?" I said no. I am not ready. I am busy sliding and climbing. Why are you grabbing me? I am not ready to go. No, NOOOOO! I am feeling so power-less, so frustrated and angry. I don't want to go and now all I can do is tell you with my body. You yell "Stop it!" I can't once the feelings are this strong, I can't, I can't just stop.

I wish those bad feelings wouldn't come. I don't choose to feel that way. It just happens, like when you come to pick me up at Hallie's house and I'm not ready to come home, or when I want a cookie and you say no or when I'm really tired. My bad feelings make you feel bad, too.

PLEASE HELP ME STOP THE BAD FEELINGS.
IT WOULD HELP IF YOU WOULD:

Let me make some decisions
about what I do.

When you say "Are you ready to go?" it sounds like you are giving me a choice. But then you say we are going. I am a person, please listen to me, I need to have some control over what I do. Instead of just telling me it's time to go, tell me we have five minutes and ask me what is the last thing I want to do before we leave the park. That way I can decide what I will do in the time that is left. Then ask me if I want to race to the car or hop like a bunny.

Please say yes.

The word *no* sets off a lot of strong feelings. Sometimes you say no, like no cookies when we are in the grocery store, and then after I scream you give me the cookie. Stop doing that! Don't just always say no to my requests, listen and say yes. I need to trust that you will listen to my ideas. Having heard yes during the day makes it easier for me to accept the nos. And I need to trust that no means no. If I think that there's a chance that you will change no to yes with a little screaming, I will try.

Let me borrow some of your control.

It feels so scary when I lose control, like I will never feel okay again. At first I can't hear anything. I know my screaming makes you angry, but please don't leave me, or yell, I need your help. Tell me in your calm voice "I know, I know you're angry, it is okay, you will be okay." If I am so upset that I am hitting you, tell me "It is not okay to hit, it is okay to be angry but it is not okay to hit." Tell me that you are trying to help me get in control but that if I hit you, you will have to step out of the room for a few minutes. It is so hard to get in control. I may need to yell and cry for a while to let the bad feelings out. Help me end my tantrum by saying "It is time to get calm and I am going to help you." Ask me if it would help if we rocked in the rocking chair, went outside to blow some bubbles, or played with some Play-Doh. Tell me that all of these help you when you need to get rid of angry feelings. Thanks for being there for me, the tough times are hard to handle alone.

TATTLING

Mommy, Greg hit me. Mommy, Greg took a cookie. Mommy, Greg made a mean face at me. Mommy, Greg is going to jump off the deck.

I follow the rules. Greg does not. I want to be sure you know that Greg is being bad and that I am not. I like it when you yell at Greg and he has to go to his room. Sometimes you yell at me, though, when I tell on Greg. You say "I don't want to hear it." He says I am a "tattletale." I don't like it when he calls me names. I'm telling Mommy!

I'M CONFUSED. WHEN SHOULD I TELL YOU IF GREG IS DOING SOMETHING BAD? I NEED YOU TO:

Teach me the telling rule.

If Greg is hitting me what should I do? He is a lot bigger than me and I need you to protect me. Will I get in trouble if I tell you? I need you to tell me that if Greg or anyone else is hurting me or someone else you want me to tell. If Greg is breaking a rule but not hurting himself or anyone I am not to

176

tell. I would only be getting Greg in trouble. It is not my job to be sure the rules are enforced, that is the grown-ups' job.

I will need some help understanding this rule, so give me a few examples. Ask me "When Greg is hitting you, is someone getting hurt?" Yes, I am getting hurt, so I should tell. "If Greg jumps off the deck is he hurting someone?" Yes, he could get hurt. Always tell a grown-up if someone is doing something that is dangerous. "If Greg takes a cookie is someone getting hurt?" No, I won't tell. What if Greg makes a face at me? I don't like it and it hurts my feelings. What should I do?

TELEPHONE

Do you like the phone more than me?

I am hungry. "Not now," you say, "I am on the phone. I'll be done in a minute." But I am hungry now! Mommy, I need to go to the potty. I don't understand the phone, I know that it makes a ringing sound and then you stop playing with me to pick it up. Then you talk to it and don't pay any attention to me. How come you get angry at me when you are talking to the phone? Can't you stop talking to it? I can stop talking to my toy phone anytime I want.

SOME WAYS YOU CAN WORK WITH ME ON
THIS INCLUDE:

Explain how the phone works.

Ask me if I would like to help you make a phone call. Tell me that we can use the phone to call Bridget's mom. We will push special numbers on our phone that will make the phone in Bridget's house ring. If they are home and pick up their phone we can talk to them. The phone lets us talk to people who are far away. Let's see if Bridget would like to come over and play.

Before we call explain that you will push the numbers, listen for Bridget's mom to answer, and say hello and your name. Then I will get a turn to talk. Tell me to talk in a medium voice and to say "Hello, this is Amanda, can Bridget come over to play?" After I say that then it will be your turn again and I am to give you back the phone. When you get done talking to Bridget's mom, I will get one more turn to talk, to say good-bye. Okay, let's try it.

Now that I know how to use the phone I will want to push the buttons and call some other people, like Grandma. You will need to tell me that I can pretend to use the phone with my toy phone but that the white phone is only for grown-ups to use. If I need to call someone I am to let you know and we can make the call together. Be sure and put the phone where I can't reach it easily, that way my curiosity won't get me in trouble.

Let the answering machine get it.

There are some times when I need your attention, like when we get home from preschool, in the morning when I'm waking up, and at dinnertime. I really like it when the phone rings and you say we'll let the answering machine get it, that we are busy. I wish you would let the answering machine

get the phone when you are playing dolls with me.
I love it when we get to play with no interruptions.
Don't you ever get tired of the phone?

Please be done in a minute.

Before you make a call say "I need to make a phone call. Is there anything you need before I do?" Help me select a puzzle or a book to look at while you are on the phone. Let me know that when you are on the phone you are listening to another person talk and that I am not to talk to you, because you can't listen to two people at one time. But if I need your attention I can come and sit in your lap. As soon as you are finished you will be able to spend some time with me. I'm not very good at waiting and not talking, so please don't talk too long.

TELEVISION

I like Peter Pan and Sesame Street and Barney.

On *Sesame Street* today the letter is *J. J* is my special letter, my name starts with *J*. After *Sesame Street* is *Barney,* can I watch it please? I like to watch TV. There are lots of colors and sounds. You must really like TV a lot, too. You turn it on first thing in the morning. I know the routine, potty first then TV. While I watch TV you are busy doing things. Some days I can watch TV for a long time.

IF THE TELEVISION IS ON I WILL WATCH IT. I NEED YOU TO DECIDE HOW MUCH TELEVISION IS GOOD FOR ME. I'D LIKE IT IF YOU WOULD:

Turn the TV off.

You may be able to get your work done with the TV on, but I can't tune it out. When the TV is on I can't play with my blocks, look at my books, work on my puzzles, or pretend I'm a firefighter rescuing people from burning buildings. On *Sesame Street* I learn about letters and numbers, and on *Barney* I learn songs. But TV is only watching and hearing, it is not doing, and I learn the very best from doing.

Watch TV with me.

Why is that little girl sad? Did she get hurt? I see things on TV that I don't understand. I am worried about the little girl and I want to know what happened. Please sit and watch with me. We can cuddle together in the rocking chair or lie down on the sofa. I like it when you ask me if I would like to visit never-never land. I think I'll pretend Peter Pan came to my window and we flew through the air to never-never land, to a castle and then to Grandma's house. Would you like to come with us?

Make a TV rule.

I have trouble shifting from TV to playing, so I fuss when you turn the TV off. It would help if we had a rule about which programs I watched. You could tell me that the rule is the TV goes off after *Sesame Street*. Remind me a little before it's over that it is almost TV-off time. Then let me decide if I will turn it off or you. Would you play with me for a few minutes? I need your help getting started, watching TV kind of makes me tired.

TIMIDNESS

No! No! I don't want to get in the pool.
Please, Mom, don't make me!

I know it is important to you that I learn to swim, but I'm scared. So scared that my insides feel all yucky inside. Please don't let the teacher grab me, it makes me panic. And don't yell at me, it makes me more frightened. I'm sorry, I'm not like the other kids, they just jump right in. Not me, new things scare me. Meagan is a doer, she doesn't think, she just jumps in. I am a watcher. You wish I was more like Meagan. But wait until we get to be teenagers, I think you will wish Meagan was more like me!

I NEED YOUR SUPPORT AND ENCOURAGEMENT.
HERE IS WHAT I NEED YOU TO DO:

Accept me as I am.

I think I have always been cautious of new situations and things. You were the one who told me that the first time I ate solid food I spit it back at you and then wouldn't open my mouth. I still don't like foods that look or smell different from what

I'm used to. And I prefer to play at my house or in our neighborhood park, I know them both really well. You say I'm being a baby. I am not! I am being Zachery and that's just how Zachery is. I don't know why. I am not choosing to feel all yucky inside. Maybe I was just born that way.

Help me prepare.

Never put me in a situation I am not prepared for. Don't just take me to the dentist and expect that I will do okay, I will not. I can't, there are too many things I don't understand. Do you always feel comfortable in new situations? Before my first dentist appointment let's go to the library and check out all the books for kids about going to the dentist. I am sure the librarian can help us find them. The library may even have a video that shows a child at the dentist. Next I will go with you on your next visit to the dentist. Tell me what is going to happen and let me sit next to you so I can see what she's doing. Maybe the dentist can talk to me about what will happen when I come in for my appointment. They might even give me a new toothbrush, too.

Let me watch.

Before I can get in that swimming pool I need to feel confident that nothing bad is going to happen to me. You can help by reminding me how much fun I have in the bathtub pretending to be a fish. Tell me that this pool is like a big bathtub. Let me know you understand how hard it is to try new things by saying "I can see you are not sure you want to get in the water today. It is the first day and you have never had swimming lessons before. It's okay if you want to sit and watch what happens, that's fine. You can join whenever you are ready." Sit with me please. Look, they are all joining hands and playing ring-around-the-rosy in the water. Now they are blowing bubbles in the water. I think I might be able to do that. I might not make it in the pool today, but maybe next time. I think I'll see if in the bath I can blow bubbles like they did.

Don't get too discouraged if I can't overcome my fear of taking swimming lessons. I might not be ready. Continuing to take me to lessons will only make me feel like a failure, and probably make you angry. Instead you come swimming with me and help me get used to the pool and the water. I would feel better if you were with me, holding on to me. Then maybe when I'm four or five I will be ready to try lessons again.

TOILET TRAINING (ACCIDENTS)

Why did I wet my pants at preschool?
I don't know.

Before I started preschool I used the potty all the time. I am a big girl and I wear big-girl underpants. Wetting my pants feels yucky. I didn't want to tell the teacher but I had to. I needed some dry clothes. She had a sad look on her face. You got a mad look on your face when she told you. I'm sorry, Mommy, I didn't mean to wet my pants. I don't really know why it happened.

*I WANT TO BE DRY! HERE IS HOW YOU CAN HELP
ME WITH THIS:*

Be calm and reassuring.

Please don't ask me what happened, I don't know and it scares me when you ask me why. And please don't yell or say "No treats for you tonight." I feel bad enough without you scolding me. You think I chose to wet my pants. I didn't! I want to be a good girl. Your reaction makes me even more upset inside, and then it's harder to stay dry. I need you to help me feel better, not so scared about using the potty. If you said something like "Oh! you had an accident, I'm sure that didn't feel very good" I would feel better. I would feel even better if you would give me a hug. It's been a hard day.

Help me feel in control.

I like my new school, so many fun things to do. The only problem is that everything is new, the room, the schedule, the teachers, and the potty. My problems at school may be because I am so busy that I don't feel when my body needs to go. Or maybe I don't feel comfortable asking a teacher to take me to the potty. Or maybe it's that the potty is big, and cold, with doors that I don't know how to use. It would help if you told me that I might be having accidents at preschool because going potty there is new to me. Come with me into the potty and talk with me about how it is different from our potty at home. Explain to me how things work and suggest that I use it before you leave. Tell me that as I get used to this school I will get used to the schedule, the teachers, and the potty, and it will be easier for me to remember to use the potty when I need to. Remind me that the teachers want to know if I need to use the potty so I don't need to be afraid to tell them.

TOILET TRAINING (HOLDING BACK BOWEL MOVEMENTS)

It's easy to pee in the potty. Pee comes out easy, poop doesn't. You tell me to push the poop out, but when I push it hurts.

It was so much easier when I wore diapers. The poop never hurt, it just came when it wanted to. Now you want me to make it come, but I can't. You say "Don't be silly, your body needs to poop. Going poop in the potty doesn't hurt." You are wrong, it does hurt. I hold it in because I don't want to hurt. Don't tell me what other children do. I am me and I work on my own schedule. I don't really understand, and what I don't understand scares me.

I WISH THERE WAS NO SUCH THING AS POOP. I NEED YOU TO:

Talk to my doctor.

When my poops finally do come out they are big and hard. Maybe the doctor knows what we can do to make them soft like when I was a baby. If the doctor tells me I need to drink lots of water and

189

juice and eat cereal I will do it. Make sure the doctor tells me why I need to eat these, I like to know, it is my body.

Let me poop in a diaper.

Sometimes I feel like I might need to poop, but when I sit on the potty no poop comes. You tell me to push, but I can't get it to come. I am having trouble knowing when I really need to go and then making it come out. It's not as easy as you say! I don't want to give up my big-boy underpants and I don't like poop in them. It might help if you let me put on my diaper just for when I think I might need to poop. That way I could work on the knowing when, without having to work on the pushing out. The diaper makes me feel safe. After the poop comes out in the diaper, please help me get cleaned up. I don't like the way it feels. Then let me put my big-boy underpants back on. Please don't get angry, tell me you know that I'm learning how to make the poop come, everyone has to do that. Let me know that before long I'll be ready to use the potty for both my poop and my pee.

Whining

You could give me everything I want and I would continue to ask for more because I guess what I really need is you.

I had a busy day at preschool today. I worked hard decorating the classroom for Halloween, and Nathan and I rode bikes as fast as we could around the gym. "Mom, I need a drink of water." "Mom, will you get me an ice cream bar." "Mom, open this box of Play-Doh." "This stupid mold won't work!" "Mom, would you do this for me?" "I need some more water!"

You tell me to stop whining, that my tone of voice really hurts your ears. But when I'm hungry and tired, whining seems to be what comes naturally.

WHAT I REALLY NEED IS FOR YOU TO:

Stop and give me your attention.

I'm tired, if you sat with me for a few minutes and did Play-Doh I would feel better. Better yet, we could rock in the rocking chair while we talked about the best and worst things that happened during the day. I'm not really big enough to be on my own, but don't tell. Hugging really helps when I'm tired, and I haven't had much time with you. Then I could help you fix dinner.

Teach me how you would like me to ask for your attention.

You have told me how not to ask for something— "Stop whining!" I'm not really sure what whining is. Tell me the words you would like me to say. You could say "It hurts my ears when I hear 'Mom, open this Play-Doh.' My ears like to hear a nicer tone of voice and words like 'Mom, please open this Play-Doh, it's stuck.'" Another option that might be even more fun is "Most wonderful Mom, please help me with this Play-Doh."

Respond to my requests.

If you can't get what I asked for right away, let me know. If you don't answer me, I assume you didn't hear me and I will ask again and again. Sometimes I ask in my polite voice and you do not respond until I use my whining voice. If you just look up and say "I hear you and I will get your water after I get done putting the potatoes in the oven," I will be able to wait (as long as it's not too long).

I don't like it when the answer is no to my requests. Sometimes it helps to explain why. "It is almost dinnertime, we don't eat ice cream bars right before dinner." I'd like it even better if you told me, "I appreciate how nicely you asked for the ice cream, we can't have it now, it's almost dinnertime, but you can have one after your bath."

WHY

When I was two my favorite word was no,
now my favorites are why, if, and how.

When I was a baby I didn't know many words, I had to touch and see things to learn about them. But now I have lots of words and I can think about things I can't even see. I use *why* when I'm trying to understand things around me. Why can't I eat my cookie on the sofa? Why do birds eat worms? How do they know where they are? If I get to eat three cookies because I'm three does that mean I will get to eat twelve cookies when I'm twelve? Why can I see the moon during the day? Why do I have to go to bed? Why do you have to go to work? Sometimes I use *why* when I just want your attention. Most of the time *why* will get you to stop what you're doing and talk to me. I like that. I learn a lot from you. But other times you get angry and say "Because I say so!" Why are you angry?

I AM USING WORDS TO LEARN ABOUT MY WORLD.
IT WOULD HELP IF YOU WOULD:

Tell me why!

I am excited about words and ideas. I want to learn about everything. Isn't that good? With your help I can learn lots of things. If you tell me the reason we don't eat cookies on the sofa is because cookie crumbs make a stain, then I will understand. It's easier to remember a rule when you know why. I am a good thinker. It's okay if you don't know the answer. Can we go to the library and get a book about birds? I have a lot of questions about birds. If you take the time to talk with me now, I will trust that you will be there for me when I'm older and have even tougher questions.

What I like the most is being and talking with you. If your brain gets tired of thinking, it's okay to tell me no more *whys* until after nap. Could we sit and cuddle?

Ask me why.

At times I ask questions that I know the answers to. It makes me feel good to know that I am right. And I really like it when you ask me questions, that helps me to think for myself. You could ask "What do you think will happen if we put this ice cube in your bathwater? Why?" Okay, let's try it.

Don't wait for me to ask why.

I hang out in the garage when you are working on the car, follow you into the bathroom when you shave, and watch you make pancakes. Please tell me what you are doing. Better yet, let me help. I can help you polish the car, and I'd like to try to pour a pancake on the griddle. It would be really cool if you would put a blob of shaving cream on my hand. I like to learn.